Ancient Peoples and Places

THE
SARMATIANS

General Editor

DR GLYN DANIEL

ABOUT THE AUTHOR

Polish-born Tadeusz Sulimirski studied at the University of Lwów, where he earned his doctorate in Prehistory and Anthropology. In 1931 he became Associate Professor of Prehistory there, a post which he held until 1936 when he was appointed Professor of Prehistoric Archaeology at the Jagiellonian University of Cracow. He left Poland in 1939 and in 1941 became Secretary General of the then Polish Ministry of Education in London. In 1958 he was appointed Special Lecturer on Central and East European Archaeology at the University of London's Institute of Archaeology. Between 1952 and 1965, the year of his official retirement, he gave lectures and held seminars in many European countries, and as recently as 1968–69 was lecturing at various universities in the United States.

Professor Sulimirski is the author of several books on Polish and Russian prehistory and a frequent contributor to a variety of learned journals. He is an Honorary Fellow of the Society of Antiquaries in London and of the Royal Anthropological Institute of Great Britain and Ireland, and is a Member of the Prehistoric Society, London-Cambridge.

THE
SARMATIANS

T. Sulimirski

60 PHOTOGRAPHS
75 LINE DRAWINGS
12 MAPS
1 CHRONOLOGICAL TABLE

 THAMES AND HUDSON

THIS IS VOLUME SEVENTY-THREE IN THE SERIES

Ancient Peoples and Places

GENERAL EDITOR: DR GLYN DANIEL

CONTENTS

ILLUSTRATIONS

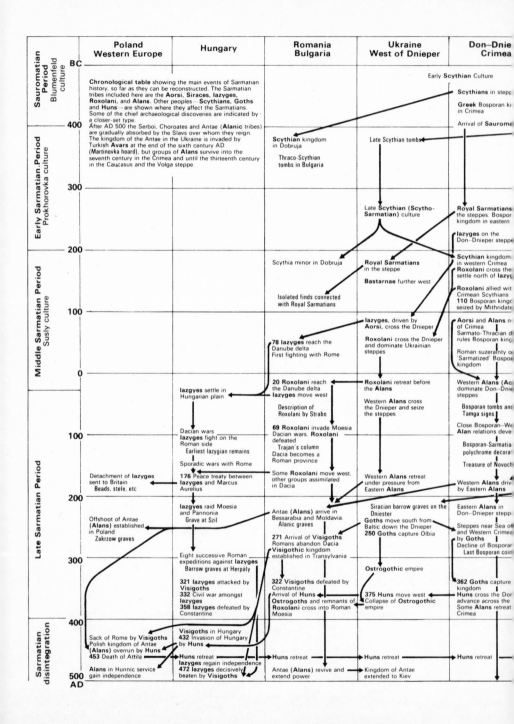

Chronological table showing the main events of Sarmatian history, so far as they can be reconstructed. The Sarmatian tribes included here are the **Aorsi, Siraces, Iazyges, Roxolani,** and **Alans.** Other peoples—**Scythians, Goths** and **Huns**—are shown where they affect the Sarmatians. Some of the chief archaeological discoveries are indicated by a closer-set type.

After AD 500 the Serboi, Choroates and Antae (**Alanic** tribes) are gradually absorbed by the Slavs over whom they reign. The kingdom of the Antae in the Ukraine is invaded by Turkish **Avars** at the end of the sixth century AD (Martinovka hoard), but groups of **Alans** survive into the seventh century in the Crimea and until the thirteenth century in the Caucasus and the Volga steppe.

Period labels (left axis):

- Sauromatian Period — Blumenfeld culture
- Early Sarmatian Period — Prokhorovka culture
- Middle Sarmatian Period — Susly culture
- Late Sarmatian Period
- Sarmatian disintegration

Time axis: BC · 400 · 300 · 200 · 100 · 0 · 100 · 200 · 300 · 400 · 500 AD

Poland / Western Europe

- Detachment of **Iazyges** sent to Britain. Beads, stele, etc
- Offshoot of Antae (**Alans**) established in Poland. Zakrzow graves
- Sack of Rome by **Visigoths**. Polish kingdom of Antae (**Alans**) overrun by Huns
- 453 Death of Attila
- **Alans** in Hunnic service gain independence

Hungary

- **Iazyges** settle in Hungarian plain
- Dacian wars. **Iazyges** fight on the Roman side. Earliest Iazygian remains. Sporadic wars with Rome
- 176 Peace treaty between **Iazyges** and Marcus Aurelius
- **Iazyges** raid Moesia and Pannonia. Grave at Szil
- Eight successive Roman expeditions against **Iazyges**. Barrow graves at Herpály
- 321 Iazyges attacked by Visigoths
- 332 Civil war amongst Iazyges
- 358 Iazyges defeated by Constantine
- Visigoths in Hungary
- 432 Invasion of Hungary by Huns
- **Huns** retreat. **Iazyges** regain independence
- 472 **Iazyges** decisively beaten by Visigoths

Romania / Bulgaria

- Scythian kingdom in Dobruja. Thraco-Scythian tombs in Bulgaria
- Scythia minor in Dobruja
- Isolated finds connected with Royal Sarmatians
- 78 **Iazyges** reach the Danube delta. First fighting with Rome
- 20 **Roxolani** reach the Danube delta. **Iazyges** move west. Description of Roxolani by Strabo
- 69 **Roxolani** invade Moesia. Dacian wars. **Roxolani** defeated. Trajan's column. Dacia becomes a Roman province
- Some **Roxolani** move west, other groups assimilated in Dacia
- Antae (**Alans**) arrive in Bessarabia and Moldavia. Alanic graves
- 271 Arrival of Visigoths. Romans abandon Dacia. Visigothic kingdom established in Transylvania
- 322 Visigoths defeated by Constantine. Arrival of Huns
- Ostrogoths and remnants of Roxolani cross into Roman Moesia
- Antae (**Alans**) revive and extend power

Ukraine West of Dnieper

- Late Scythian tombs
- Late Scythian (Scytho-Sarmatian) culture
- **Royal Sarmatians** in the steppe. **Bastarnae** further west
- **Iazyges**, driven by Aorsi, cross the Dnieper. **Roxolani** cross the Dnieper and dominate Ukrainian steppes
- **Roxolani** retreat before the Alans. Western **Alans** cross the Dnieper and seize the steppes
- Western **Alans** retreat under pressure from Eastern **Alans**
- Siracian barrow graves on the Dniester. **Goths** move south from Baltic down the Dnieper. 250 Goths capture Olbia
- Ostrogothic empire
- 375 Huns move west. Collapse of Ostrogothic empire
- **Huns** retreat
- Kingdom of Antae extended to Kiev

Don–Dnie(per) / Crimea

- Early **Scythian** Culture
- **Scythians** in steppe
- **Greek** Bosporan ki(ngdom) in Crimea
- Arrival of **Sauroma(tians)**
- **Royal Sarmatians** the steppes. Bospor(an) kingdom in eastern
- **Iazyges** on the Don–Dnieper steppe
- **Scythian** kingdom in western Crimea. **Roxolani** cross the settle north of Iazy(ges)
- **Roxolani** allied wit(h) Crimean Scythians. 110 Bosporan king(dom) seized by Mithridate(s)
- **Aorsi** and **Alans** n(orth) of Crimea. Sarmato-Thracian d(ynasty) rules Bosporan king(dom). Roman suzerainty o(ver) 'Sarmatized' Bospor(an) kingdom
- Western **Alans** (Ao) dominate Don–Dnie(per) steppes. Bosporan tombs and Tamga signs
- Close Bosporan–We(stern) **Alan** relations deve(lop). Bosporan-Sarmatia(n) polychrome decora(tion). Treasure of Novoch(erkassk)
- Western **Alans** driv(en) by Eastern **Alans**
- Eastern **Alans** in Don–Dnieper steppe
- Steppes near Sea of (Azov) and Western Crimea by **Goths**. Decline of Bosporan. Last Bosporan coin
- 362 Goths capture (Bosporan) kingdom. **Huns** cross the Don, advance across the Some **Alans** retreat Crimea
- **Huns** retreat

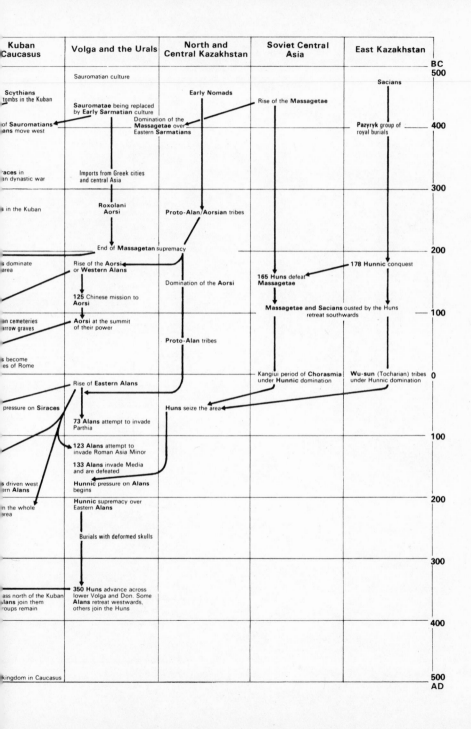

Kuban Caucasus	Volga and the Urals	North and Central Kazakhstan	Soviet Central Asia	East Kazakhstan	

BC 500

Sauromatian culture

Sacians

Scythians tombs in the Kuban

Early Nomads

Rise of the **Massagetae**

Sauromatae being replaced by **Early Sarmatian** culture

of **Sauromatians** ans move west

Domination of the **Massagetae** over Eastern **Sarmatians**

Pazyryk group of royal burials **400**

aces in an dynastic war

Imports from Greek cities and central Asia

300

s in the Kuban

Roxolani Aorsi

Proto-Alan/Aorsian tribes

End of Massagetan supremacy **200**

s dominate area

Rise of the **Aorsi** or **Western Alans**

178 Hunnic conquest

165 Huns defeat Massagetae

Domination of the **Aorsi**

125 Chinese mission to **Aorsi**

Massagetae and Sacians ousted by the Huns retreat southwards

an cemeteries arrow graves

Aorsi at the summit of their power **100**

Proto-Alan tribes

s become es of Rome

Kangiui period of **Chorasmia** under **Hunnic** domination

Wu-sun (Tocharian) tribes under Hunnic domination **0**

Rise of **Eastern Alans**

pressure on **Siraces**

Huns seize the area

73 Alans attempt to invade Parthia

100

123 Alans attempt to invade Roman Asia Minor

133 Alans invade Media and are defeated

s driven west ern **Alans**

Hunnic pressure on **Alans** begins

Hunnic supremacy over Eastern **Alans** **200**

n the whole area

Burials with deformed skulls

300

ass north of the Kuban lans join them roups remain

350 Huns advance across lower Volga and Don. Some **Alans** retreat westwards, others join the Huns

400

kingdom in Caucasus

500 AD

Foreword

THE SARMATIANS HAVE received scant attention since the days of the classical and medieval writers, and have long been numbered among the forgotten peoples of antiquity. Now, however, thanks mainly to archaeological work carried out during the past few decades in the steppe-lands east of the Volga, in the Ukraine and in Hungary, it has become possible to reconstruct, at least in part, the story of these once powerful nomadic peoples stemming from Eastern Europe. The few books on the subject that have so far appeared deal with particular periods and limited areas, while the excavation reports are confined to specialist journals. This is the first general work on the Sarmatians—known at a later stage in their history mainly under the name of the Alans—to have been attempted so far.

Sarmatian-Alanic history has a time-span of well over a millennium, and was played out on a vast stage nearly 3,000 miles across, from the Altai Mountains in Siberia westwards to the Carpathians; and, if we include the history of splinter groups, this stage must be extended westwards as far as France, Spain and even the British Isles, and eastwards up to the East China Sea. The Sarmatians—a term which we shall use in future to include also the Alanic element—never cohered into a political entity, and the culture of their many tribes and groups always differed to some extent from one to the other. Any reconstruction of their history that does not take this into account is bound to present a distorted picture.

The story of the Sarmatians is one of many tribes and groups migrating from east to west, each pushing forward and being pushed in turn from behind, until they reached the barrier of Rome, whereupon they broke into yet more complex eddies and cross-currents. Each group, on arriving in fresh surroundings, tended to maintain its ancient culture, rites and customs, even though back in the homeland from which it had been driven new developments were already taking place.

It is possible to distinguish five main periods in Sarmatian history, by the end of which the character of the people had undergone radical changes. This division into periods is based on changing conditions and evolutionary trends in the ancient Sarmatian nuclear domain, the lower Volga steppe, changes which, in turn, were determined by the sequence of events in the steppe-lands of Asia further to the east—a process which also applies to a lesser degree in the countries west of the Volga.

These periods, to which the terminology established by Soviet archaeologists has been applied, are treated in sequence in the chapters that follow. In the introductory chapter the general character of the Sarmatians is discussed, the kind of life they led and the manner in which they organized their affairs. The second chapter deals with the earliest period in their history, covering the sixth and fifth centuries BC, known as the 'Sauromatian period' in the west, and in the steppe-lands of the Volga and Urals, and as the 'period of the Early Nomads' in the Asian steppes. The next three chapters describe the ensuing 'Early', 'Middle', and 'Late' Sarmatian periods, covering between them some eight hundred years up to the fourth century AD, by which time Central Europe had come within their sphere of activity. The Epilogue records briefly how the Sarmatians were dispersed all over Europe, became absorbed by other peoples and eventually lost their identity.

In reconstructing, in broad outline, the very complicated and involved history of the various Sarmatian-Alanic groups, I have attempted to knit together all the relevant accounts of ancient and early medieval writers, and to interpret the related archaeo-logical material accordingly. A Chronological Table shows the main trends in the westward migrations of the principal Sarma-tian-Alan peoples during the consecutive periods of their common history, and this shifting of the Sarmatian field of activity from east to west is illustrated in a number of maps.

In writing this book I have availed myself of the numerous excavation reports on Sarmatian-Alan sites and consulted works dealing with individual stages in the history of these peoples; the most important are listed in the bibliography at the end of the volume. Thanks to grants from the Pilgrim Fund of the British Academy, to whom my grateful thanks are due, I was able to study relevant material in a number of museums in the USSR, Romania, Hungary, Austria, Germany and France. Very rewarding, too, were my discussions with such leading authorities in Sarmatian-Alan archaeology as Dr M. Párducz in Budapest; Professor K. Horedt and Mr I. H. Crişan in Cluj, Romania; Messrs Gh. Diaconu, B. Mitrea and S. Morintz of the Institute of Archaeology of the Romanian Academy in Bucharest; Professor B. A. Rybakov, Director of the Institute of Archaeology of the Academy of Sciences of the USSR in Moscow, and Dr K. F. Smirnov of the same Institute; Messrs S. S. Chernikov, V. P. Shilov and Iu. A. Zadneprovskii of the Institute of Archaeology of the Academy of Sciences of the USSR in Leningrad; M. J. J. Hatt, Director or the Musée Archéologique in Strasbourg; M. E. Salin in Nancy-Laneveville, and Abbé A. Nouel in Orleans. I am also much indebted to Mmes A. P. Mantsevich and K. M. Skalon, Keepers of the Scythian and Sarmatian Departments of the Hermitage Museum in Leningrad, and Mrs N. V. Pyatisheva, Keeper of the Scytho-Sarmatian Department of the Historical Museum in Moscow; Mr K. A. Velichko, Director of the Provincial Museum in Rostov-on-the-Don; Dr A. Mozsolics and Dr M. Párducz of the Magyar Nemzeti Museum in Budapest; Professor V. Dumitrescu, Director of the Archaeological Museum in Bucharest; Professor M. Petrescu-Dimboviţa, Iaşi; Mr J. Antonescu, Director of the Bacău Museum; Professor O. Doppelfeld, Director of the

Römisch-Germanisches Museum in Cologne; Professor H.-J. Hundt of the Römisch-Germanisches Zentral Museum in Mainz; Mlle C. Metzger of the Musée des Antiquités Nationales at St Germain-en-Laye; and Mlle M. Dubisson, Conservateur du Musée des Beaux Arts in Troyes, for their willing assistance while I was studying materials under their care; and also to all my fellow archaeologists in the museums I visited. I have also to express my thanks for their kind help to Miss J. du Plat Taylor and Miss G. C. Talbot, M.A., Librarians of the University of London Institute of Archaeology; Miss B. J. Kirkpatrick, Librarian of the Royal Anthropological Institute, and to Mr J. Hopkins, Librarian of the Society of Antiquaries of London. I am indebted to Mrs E. Rhys for correcting and improving my English text.

Finally, I wish to express my gratitude to the Institutes of Archaeology of the Academy of Sciences of the USSR in Moscow and in Leningrad; to the Musée Départemental des Antiquités in Rouen; to the Musée des Beaux-Arts, Troyes; to the Muzeum Narodowe and Państwowe Muzeum Archeologiczne, both in Warsaw, and to the Nemzeti Museum, Budapest, for supplying me with a series of photographs.

T. S.

CHAPTER I

Introduction

IDENTIFYING THE SARMATIANS

MORE THAN HALF of the Fourth Book of the *Histories* of Herodotus, the Greek writer of the fifth century BC, is devoted to a description of Scythia, modern Ukraine, and its inhabitants, the nomad Scythians. But Herodotus, who must have met the Scythians during his stay in Olbia, then the main Greek city-colony on the northern Black Sea coast, also gave his attention to several neighbouring peoples, among them the Sauromatians—the Greek version of the Roman name Sarmatians.

When they appear on the stage of history, the Sarmatians lived close to the eastern border of ancient Scythia. Herodotus (IV, 21), who is the first to mention them, says that 'after one crosses the River Tanais [the Don] it is no longer Scythia, but the first region belongs to the Sauromatians who, beginning from Lake Maeotis [the Sea of Azov], occupy the country northwards, for fifteen days' journey, all destitute of wild and cultivated trees.' Hippocrates (460–377 BC), another early Greek author, also places them near the Sea of Azov, and according to Strabo (XI, 2, 2), little is known of the country on the Tanais 'because of the coldness and the poverty of the country'.

Archaeological research during the last forty years has shown *Fig. 1* that the territory of the early Sarmatians also embraced the southern Urals and the steppe-land east of the River Ural. But the archaeological remains in the huge territories further to the east, the steppe country of Kazakhstan as far as the Altai Mountains and parts of Central Asia, also resemble those of the Sauromatians of the southern Urals and the lower Volga, suggesting that these areas were at that time inhabited by peoples closely related to the Sauromatians. Most of them are clearly ancestral to the various

21

Sarmatian tribes which later moved westwards into the North Pontic area, where their presence and tribal names were subse-quently recorded by the ancients.

Conditions in the steppe country of Asia were never stable in antiquity and tribal movements are reported from the very distant past. The adoption, or invention, of horse-riding and the evolution of mounted archers—probably by the middle of the second millennium BC—was the turning point in the history of these peoples. The pastoral nomads, mounted on swift horses, and trained to warfare from their early childhood, became a real menace to their neighbours and to peoples who lived far outside the steppe belt.

There was constant minor friction between the steppe tribes: major wars, sometimes caused by drought and often by external factors would, from time to time, impel a large group to seek new pastures at the expense of their neighbours, thus causing further disturbances. So various Sarmatian tribes, pushed by their eastern neighbours, moved successively to the Black Sea steppes, and then further west, yielding to pressure from the oncoming wave. Both historical and archaeological evidence enable us to trace the movements of most of their tribes and groups in Europe. The ultimate fate of all those who moved west was more or less the same: sooner or later they were absorbed into the native population which they conquered or among which they settled.

SARMATIAN TRIBES

The Sarmatians were of Indo-European stock belonging to the northern branch of the Iranian-speaking group, often called the Scythian group of peoples, which included the Sacians of Soviet Central Asia. They were closely akin to the ancient Medes, Parthians and Persians. Their language was related to that of the Avesta and—at least that of Herodotus' Sauromatians, their westernmost branch—is considered to have been a dialect of the Scythian tongue, theirs being the more archaic of the two.

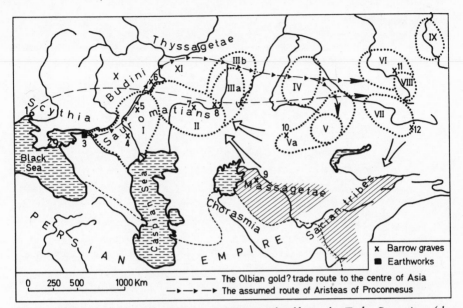

Fig. 1 Cultures of the sixth-fifth centuries BC attributable to the Early Sarmatians (the Sauromatians of Herodotus) and neighbouring peoples in Europe, and to the proto-Sarmatians (the 'Early Nomads') of the Kazakhstan steppe (after K. F. Smirnov, Tolstov and Komarova) I Lower Volga group; II Samara-Ural group; IIIa Cheliabinsk group, b Andronovo culture of the Bronze Age (the Ircae); IV North Kazakhstan group ('other Scythians'); V Central Kazakhstan group of the Andronovo culture (the Issedonians), Va 'Early Nomad' finds of the Scythian period; VI Upper Ob group of the Andronovo culture, the Maiemirskaya culture of the Scythian period and the Bolsherechenskaya culture (the Argippaei ?); VII Area of distribution of East Kazakhstan Andronovo finds and 'Early Nomad' remains (the Arimaspians ?); VIII Pazyryk group of the Scythian culture; IX Tagarskaya culture (the Tocharians ?); X Gorodetskaya culture (the Budini); XI Ananino culture (the Thyssagetae); 1 Olbia; 2 Kerch-Panticapaeum; 3 Elisavetovskoe earthwork; 4 Solenoe Zaimishche barrow grave; 5 Blumenfeld barrow grave cemetery; 6 Staryi Pecheur; 7 Pyatimary and Ak-Bulak cemeteries; 8 Bish-Oba; 9 Uygarak barrow graves; 10 Dyndy-Bay; 11 Berezovka cemetery; 12 Chiliktinskii barrow grave

The Sarmatians were never a homogeneous people and consisted of several tribes whose names are recorded by the ancients, and who differed to some extent from each other. It is a mistake, therefore, to treat all the Sarmatians alike, as has often been done, with the result that some special practices and features character, istic of one branch only, e.g. cranial deformation, have been presented as typical of all the Sarmatian peoples. We may assume that each main Sarmatian group spoke its own dialect, although nothing is known about these because of the complete absence of any written texts. But the language of the Ossetinians in the central Caucasus, which evolved out of ancient Sarmatian, Alan dialects, can be considered as a kind of modern Sarmatian.

The first Sarmatian people to be known by name were those referred to as Surmatai or Syrmatai in some ancient records. The name was subsequently applied by the ancients to the whole group of kindred tribes and peoples of whom the mightiest were probably the Alans (Alani), whose name later supplanted the ancient term 'Sarmatians' to denote the whole eastern group of the people. Some authors consider the Alans to have been a people distinct from the Sarmatians, although of the same stock.

Other Sarmatian peoples who asserted themselves were the Iazyges, Roxolani, Siraces, Aorsi and the Antae. No names have come down to us of the Sarmatian-Alan peoples during their stay in their original country, the steppes of Asia, except the two or three names of large tribal units mentioned in the account of the journey of Aristeas of Proconnesus by Herodotus (IV, 13–27).

The mixed character of the Sarmatians has been revealed by the ancient pictographic material and by anthropological studies of skeletal remains, mainly cranial. Most frequently encountered in the Kazakhstan steppe country is the so-called 'Andronovo' racial type; brachycephalic, Europoid; which shows clearly that the majority of the people were descended from Bronze Age Andronovians. Skulls of this type have also been found on the lower Volga where, at least in the earlier periods of Sarmatian history, the most characteristic is the 'Srubnaya' Mediterranean racial type, similarly inherited by the western Sarmatians (Herod, otus' Sauromatians) from their Bronze Age ancestors.

In the second half of the fifth century BC a new racial element appeared in the steppe region of the southern Urals. This was the 'Pamiro-Fergana' type proper to parts of Central Asia, corres-ponding to the 'Armenoid' type of Western anthropologists. During the period from the third century BC to the third century AD, it spread to the regions between the lower Volga south of Volgograd and Manych, as graves there show. Still later, by the end of the pre-Christian era, brachycephalic elements native to the west Siberian forest zone, and those with Mongoloid features, had reached the lower Volga. These changes and the appearance of eastern racial elements in the west, where they had not been recorded previously, reflect the tribal migrations of the Sarmatians.

MODE OF LIFE AND ECONOMY

The Sarmatians were steppe dwellers and most of them led a nomadic life, their economy being based on stock-breeding. Strabo says that the country was cold and poor: 'This poverty can indeed be endured by the indigenous peoples who, in nomadic fashion, live on flesh and milk, but people from other tribes

Fig. 2   Terracotta figurine from Kerch-Panticapaeum of a Sarmatian hunting hares on horseback (after Narysy)

Fig. 3   Scytho-Sarmatian clay model of a nomad wagon-dwelling, found in Kerch-Panticapaeum

Fig. 2

Fig. 3

cannot stand it.' In some parts of the country, in the vicinity of the rivers, the Sarmatians were also to a lesser degree engaged in agriculture. They also hunted whatever game was to be found.

The Sarmatian mode of life and economy was similar to that of the Scythians. According to both Herodotus and Hippocrates they had no houses, but lived in wagons. The same picture is given by Strabo (VII, 3, 4, 17, 18) about four centuries later; he reports that the tents of the Roxolani and other Sarmatian nomad tribes, 'made of felt, are fastened to the wagons (drawn by oxen) in which they spend their lives; round about the tents are the herds which provide milk, cheese, and meat on which they live.' In another passage, he mentions that they 'live on meat in general but also on horse-meat and mare's milk', fresh and sour. 'They follow the grazing herds, from time to time moving to other places that have grass.' He also mentions their seasonal migrations: they lived near the Sea of Azov in winter and in the plain in summer. Seasonal migrations were probably also a normal feature in the steppe between the Volga and the Urals, and in Kazakhstan, especially in the regions close to the mountains, where herds were moved to highland pastures for grazing in the summer. The description of the Alans, a late Sarmatian people, by Ammianus Marcellinus, writing in the fourth century AD, some 800 years after Herodotus, is almost identical. Of interest are his remarks that they placed their carts in a circle, and that they gave particular attention to breeding horses; these, like those of the Scythians, were small but exceedingly quick and hard to manage, and were therefore gelded.

No Sarmatian settlements have been found in the steppe, apart from traces of temporary encampments in a few regions. It is only on the periphery of Sarmatian territory within the forest⁄steppe zone that remains of settlements with Sarmatian finds have been discovered. They were found in the region of Kuibyshev and in parts of the southern Urals, and had belonged to peoples engaged in agricultural activities who were of mixed origin, consisting of Sarmatians who had mingled with the natives. The distaste of the true nomad Sarmatians for agricultural activities is well attested by Strabo (VII, 4, 6). A similar state of affairs had existed in the north⁄west Caucasus and the country from the north coast of the Sea of Azov to the Don. Strabo (XI, 2, 2, 1) identifies the Aorsi and Siraces, the two large Sarmatian tribes of his time, and mentions that some were nomads and some tent⁄dwellers and farmers. This has been confirmed by the results of archaeological investigation, and the same applies to the later Alans.

CHARACTER AND WARFARE

According to the descriptions of ancient authors, the Sarmatians did not differ much from the Scythians in their dress and customs; they too wore long trousers, soft leather boots and soft round or pointed caps, though some also went bare⁄headed like many Scythians. Nevertheless, there were certain differences between the Iranian nomads, the Scythians, Sarmatians and Sacians in Asia. These are well illustrated by figures of Scythians on Plates 1–3, 20 plaques, silver and gold vases and toreutics found in richly furnished tombs; Sarmatian figures depicted in Panticapaean tombs; and Sacian figures on Persian bas⁄reliefs. Archaeological investigations have revealed similar differences in the material culture, funerary rites and type of burial constructions, even among the main Sarmatian tribes whose way of life and several recorded customs and usages were almost identical—and also among individual Sarmatian tribal units, as will be seen later.

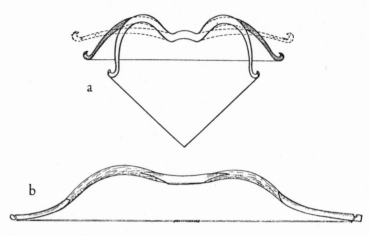

Fig. 4   Bows of the steppe peoples, a reflex bow of Scythian type; b composite bow of Hunnic type (after Khazarov)

Strabo (VII, 4.6) says of the Roxolani that 'the young men grow in the habit of riding from their earliest boyhood and regard it as contemptible to go on foot. Various forms of training make them into skilled warriors.' That this was true also of other Sarmatian tribes is indicated by a series of children's graves uncovered in various parts of the territory; these contained weapons, from which we may infer that the children were already trained in their use at an early age. In this respect the habits of the various Sarmatian tribes and peoples were much alike and remained unchanged for centuries. According to Ammianus Marcellinus (fourth century AD), 'almost all Halani [Alans] are tall and handsome, their hair inclines to blond; by the ferocity of their glance they inspire dread.... They delight in danger and warfare.'

The Sarmatians fought on horseback and also on foot. Their armament consisted of a short curved bow, which was their main weapon at an early period; a quiverful of arrows; an iron sword of *akinakes* type, longer than that of the Scythians, and of Persian or West Asiatic design, sometimes up to 130 cm long; occasionally a

Fig. 4a

Fig. 5   Wall painting in a 'catacomb' tomb at Kerch-Panticapaeum, representing a combat scene (after E. H. Minns)

light lance or spear with an iron head, and, rarely, a battle-axe. To quote Strabo on the Roxolani again, he says, 'they use helmets and corselets of raw ox-hides, carry wicker shields, and have for weapons spears, bow, and sword'. Slings and lassos were likewise used.

The Sarmatians' manner of waging war was much the same as that of the Scythians and other steppe peoples. In the early periods, they attacked the enemy with large groups of mounted bowmen, consummate horsemen who had perfected the art of shooting while at full gallop. In the second century BC the armament of some Sarmatian tribes changed radically, especially that of the Roxolani, who became the leading Sarmatian people of the North Pontic steppes. Their principal weapons were heavy, long iron-headed lances and long swords with a wooden grip. According to Strabo, the swords were of an 'enormous size which they wield with both hands'. Bows and arrows then played a secondary role. They were clad in armour made either of small iron plates sewn on leather, or of thick hide, and the

Fig. 5

Fig. 6   Sarmatians (Roxolani ?) clad in mail armour on a bas-relief of the Galerius Arch in Thessaloniki (after Rostovtsev)

horses were protected in the same manner; helmets too were made mostly of hide. At first this armour was worn only by the chiefs.

The earliest cuirasses, made of bronze scales, appear in the North Pontic area in the sixth century BC, exclusively in ancient Scythia and the north-west Caucasus.[1] In the fifth century, a few found their way into Sauromatian burials on the lower Volga. In Scythia, they were gradually supplemented by wide battle-belts similarly made of small bronze or iron plates, or of long, narrow strips sewn on leather, and armour of thick hide. These are also found in richly furnished Sarmatian graves of the Early Sarmatian period, the fourth to the second centuries BC.

Armoured cavalry was known to the Assyrians and its use must have been adopted subsequently by the Persians and Scythians, and after them by the Sauromatians on the lower Volga. Its spread into Central Asia was much more important; by the end of the fourth century BC, the Chorasmians and Massagetae had formed special units of heavy armoured cavalry, and had developed a tactical method of using it in battle.[2] The cavalry, the 'cataphracti', fought in close battle array, and no adversary could resist it. The introduction of this new tactic brought about a complete change in warfare in the east; the light mounted archers were to some extent replaced by armoured cavalry. The Chinese adopted the new method, as did the Sarmatians, especially the Roxolani, but not the Iazyges. During the Middle Sarmatian period special units of heavy cavalry, consisting mainly of the tribal nobles, were formed. Such a detachment, clad in mail, is represented on Trajan's Column fleeing before the Romans. Sarmatians serving in the Roman army, wearing scale armour, are depicted on the Arch of Galerius at Salonica (AD 297). The Sarmatians were the chief disseminators of this tactic in Eastern and Central Europe, and even the Romans were forced to equip some units in the same fashion.

Plate 4

Fig. 6

'The Roxolani have the reputation of being warlike; yet all barbarian races and lightly armed peoples are weak when matched against a well-ordered and well-armed phalanx.' Thus Strabo. According to Tacitus, individual Sarmatians were not very valiant, and were weak when fighting on foot, though their squadrons of heavy cavalry were hard to resist. He emphasizes, however, that on ice and wet ground their long lances and swords were not of much help because their horses would slip and their armour weigh them down. Strabo also remarks that while their armour is impenetrable, it was so unwieldy that 'he who falls in the battle is never able to rise again'.

Fig. 4b

The second century AD saw the decline of armoured cavalry and a change in Sarmatian tactics following the introduction of the new and formidable 'Hunnic' bow, a complex weapon reinforced with small plates of bone. Arrows with a stronger iron point shot from bows of this type were able to penetrate armour. This change was brought about by the arrival of new Sarmatian (Alan) tribes from the east, whom the occupants of the East European steppe could not withstand.

Writing of the Roxolani, Tacitus says that 'plunder not war, is their passion, a band of freebooters, determined to ravage the country,' and ancient records are full of references to Sarmatian rapine. It would seem, however, that this propensity for plunder was mainly confined to those groups of Sarmatians who had been ousted from their native steppe country by their eastern neighbours, for Strabo remarks that those who lived in the north Pontic steppe country were warriors rather than brigands.

Perhaps the most interesting of Strabo's comments (VII.7.3, 7) relate to the impact of Greek and Roman civilization on the Sarmatian nomads (whom he calls 'the Scythians'). 'We regard the Scythians,' he writes, 'as the most straightforward of men and the least prone to mischief, also as far more frugal and independent of each other than we are. And yet our mode of life has caused a change for the worse in almost all peoples, introducing amongst them luxury and sensual pleasures and, to satisfy these vices, base artifices that lead to innumerable acts of greed.'

SOCIAL ORGANIZATION, BELIEFS

The early writers say little about the social organization of the Sarmatians. It was undoubtedly similar to that of the Scythians. Ammianus Marcellinus says of the Alans that they did not have slaves, and that 'all were born of noble blood'; the same probably applies to other Sarmatian tribes, as no ancient author mentions the presence of slaves among them. Ammianus also reports that the Alans choose as chiefs 'those who are conspicuous for their long experience as warriors.' The western Sarmatian tribes of the last centuries BC and the early centuries of the Christian era, had kings, or chiefs; some of their names have come down to us.

More light is shed on the social organization of the Sarmatians by a study of their burials. We find that during the earliest stage of their history, small mounds with very modestly furnished graves were concentrated around one, or two, larger mounds, evidently those of their chiefs, who were possibly hereditary. However, the grave goods in the latter were of much the same kind as in the other burials, the quantity alone varying. The same applies to graves of this period excavated in the steppe of Kazakh, stan. But by the late fifth century BC we see a marked contrast between one grave and another both as regards the quality and the quantity of the content, many burials having no grave goods at all, while others, differently constructed, are lavishly endowed with gold and imported goods. Special cemeteries for the tribal aristocracy were also introduced.

These changes were undoubtedly the outcome of tribal move, ments and the wars and conquests to which they gave rise. The position of the successful war chiefs was thereby consolidated, while that of the defeated and subjected tribes who did not retreat before the victorious aggressors worsened. The hetero, geneous composition of the Sarmatian tribes, especially in the later periods, becomes evident from a study of the cranial material. The considerable variations in the funeral rites and construction of coeval graves forming part of the same cemetery, even though their equipment may be alike, lead us to the same conclusion.

Of particular interest is the position of women in most Sar, matian tribes, but especially among the Sauromatians as described by Herodotus (VII, 110–117). These, he claimed, were the off, spring of union between the Amazons and the Scythians. This accounts for the fact that their wives kept to 'the ancient Amazon mode of living, going out on horseback to hunt, and joining their husbands in war, wearing the same dress as men'. He also says that no virgin was permitted to marry until she had killed an enemy. Almost the same description is given by Hippocrates, who also mentions that their right breast is seared in infancy, so that it shall not hinder their right arm in fighting, when throwing the javelin or shooting with the bow. Strabo later gives a similar account of the Amazons, who in his day are said to have lived somewhere in the central part of the north Caucasian foothills, in the neighbourhood of certain Sarmatian tribes. The relatively large number of graves of armed women, especially in Sauromatian cemeteries, is usually looked upon as evidence of the survival of the ancient pre-Sauromatian social order based on a matriarchy.

Plate 5

Hippocrates maintained that Sarmatian women were not only warriors but also priestesses. Pedestalled stone 'altars',[3] or flat, rounded stone dishes with raised rims are frequently found among the grave goods in a series of female burials in cemeteries of the south Ural group during the Sauromatian period, and they have also been found in similar graves further to the east, in central Kazakhstan. These objects, often decorated in the 'Scythian' animal style, are recognized as an attribute of the women-priestesses. Several such graves were of a special construction and richly furnished, although the 'altars' and stone dishes also appear in modestly furnished graves. Bronze rings, necklaces of semi-precious stones, lumps of white, red, green and yellow paint, and often lumps of charcoal, occurred in these burials.

Fig. 7

Very little is known about the religious beliefs of the Sarmatians. They seem to have worshipped the sun as well as fire, and believed in its purificatory power. These beliefs and practices were obviously inherited from their Bronze Age, and even Neolithic, ancestors. They are well attested by traces of fires built close to graves or over them, by signs that the grave-shaft had been fired, often in connection with a partial cremation, and by lumps of charcoal thrown into the grave or strewn around it. The 'altars' of the priestesses were possibly connected with fire-

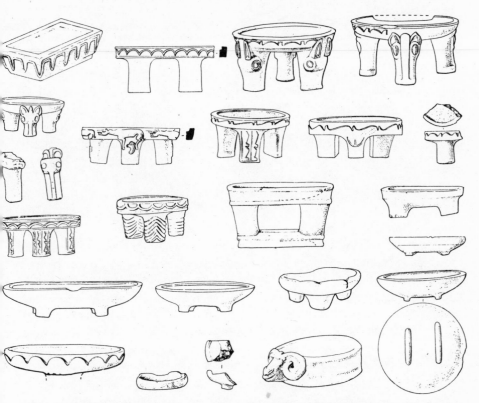

Fig. 7 *Portable stone 'altars' from Sauromatian burials, mainly of the Samara-Ural group (after Smirnov and Petrenko)*

worship. Associated with these practices was probably also the worship of the sun, or the sun-god. Later, in the Christian era, Zoroastrianism seems to have found adherents among some Sarmatian, mainly Alan, tribes.

A few other peculiarities of the Sarmatians deserve mention. For example, Ammianus Marcellinus says of the Alans that 'they have a remarkable way of divining the future. They gather very straight twigs of ozier and sort them out at an appointed time with secret incantations, and thus clearly learn what impends.' The same practice was reported by Herodotus

Plate 2

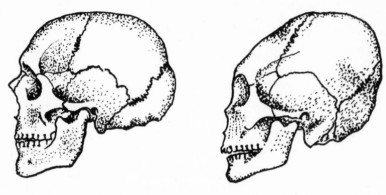

Fig. 8   Example of a deformed skull from Nieder Olm, Germany (right) contrasted with one of normal shape

(IV, 67) several centuries earlier in his description of the Scythians of the Pontic steppe.

Another enduring practice, first recorded among the Scythians of the North Pontic area, but probably also widespread among the Sarmatians, was the worship of the iron sword, the 'scimitar'. According to Herodotus (IV, 62), the sword was thought by the Scythians to be the image of Mars 'to which they bring yearly sacrifices of cattle and horses', but sometimes also human sacrifices in the form of war captives. Sword worship is reported as late as the fourth century AD by Ammianus Marcellinus, who says that the Alans worshipped—as their god of war—a naked sword fixed in the ground.

Fig. 8

A practice, often wrongly regarded as characteristic of all the Sarmatians, was the artificial deformation of skulls, effected by binding the child's head in a special manner in order to make it grow to a particular shape. It is first recorded in our area in a few graves of the Catacomb culture on the lower Volga and the Manych in the first half of the second millennium BC. But it is only among the inhabitants of the Volga steppe, the Eastern Alans, during the Late Sarmatian period (second to fourth century AD)

Fig. 9   Examples of Sauromatian-Sarmatian decorative art: talismans carved in bone, antler and boar tusk, representing rapacious and fantastic animals (after Smirnov)

that cranial deformation becomes a common custom. Up to 70 per cent of male skulls from their cemeteries are deformed. It was widely practised in Central Asia during the early Christian centuries, especially among the Huns, and was evidently adopted by the Eastern Alans when still in the Kazakhstan steppes.

The Sarmatians believed in an after-life, which they must have imagined as a continuation of their earthly life. This is reflected in their funerary rites and grave goods. The deceased had to be adequately equipped for the journey to the life beyond; men had to be accompanied by their wives and, in later periods and among some tribes, the chiefs had to be attended by serfs who were sacrificed on their graves. There is no uniformity in the funerary rites; the position occupied by the skeleton in the grave, the direction in which the head faced, and the arrangement of the grave goods all varied according to the beliefs and customs current among the different Sarmatian tribes at different periods. This will be discussed when dealing with each. Partial or total cremations were also common among some tribes at certain periods.

Other beliefs and practices, mostly of an animistic nature, are attested by finds of broken or damaged bronze mirrors deposited in graves, and by the frequency of amulets and talismans. Of interest are carved boar tusks affixed to the swords and to horse harness.

Fig. 61

Fig. 9

In the west, stelae bearing a rough image of a dead ancestor were sometimes worshipped. They were usually set up on the burial ground between the mounds, or flat graves, but seldom on the mound itself. Anthropomorphic stelae are not typical of the Sarmatians; they were adopted by the respective tribes when they arrived in the north Pontic area, after they had absorbed the remnants of their predecessors in the country.

CHAPTER II

The Sarmatian Dawn
Sixth and fifth centuries BC

THE SAUROMATIANS

THE EARLIEST Sarmatians, the 'Sauromatians' of Herodotus, inhabited the lower Volga steppe-land. A large quantity
of archaeological finds dated to the sixth and fifth centuries BC
in that region may, therefore, be safely associated with them.
They make up the so-called 'Sauromatian culture', and the
period is known as the 'Sauromatian period'.[1]

However, other closely related archaeological finds have been
discovered over a much wider area, extending north and north-
east over the grassland east of the Volga, south of Kuibyshev and
across the south Ural steppes. They imply that another branch of
the people lived in the south Urals; their territory probably extended even further eastwards, but so far this limit has not been
established. To the east, in the huge steppe country of Kazakhstan, and the northern part of Soviet Central Asia, lived several
allied peoples and tribes to whom the designation 'Early Nomads'
has recently been given in Soviet archaeological literature; they
are also known as the 'Eastern Scythians'. In fact, the Sauromatian culture formed the westernmost outpost of this group,
whose territory covered some 3,000 km. between the Don and the
Volga in the west, and the Altai Mountains in the east.

Nearly 500 Sauromatian burials have been found. They are
divided into two distinct groups called the Lower Volga group,
and the Samara-Ural group. The differences between the two
groups are reflected in their burial rites, grave goods and, to some
extent, their racial composition as revealed by a study of the
cranial material; these differences can be accounted for by the fact
that the one group developed from the Srubnaya culture on the

Volga, and the other from the Andronovo culture in the east, even though there was a considerable mingling of these two Bronze Age groups before the emergence of the Sauromatian culture.

No settlements attributable to the Sauromatians have been found, only traces of a few temporary encampments; graves in mounds are almost the only archaeological evidence we have. These are mostly secondary burials in mounds of the preceding periods, less than one-third being primary burials under mounds. Earth mounds are typical of the Volga group, whereas those of the Samara-Ural group are mostly built of stone, or have a cairn over the grave. Stone rings around the graves have been discovered in the Urals, and also anthropomorphic stelae. The *Fig. 10* grave-shafts are mostly narrow, but some, usually better furnished and evidently belonging to important persons in Sauromatian society, are nearly square in plan. Many are timber-lined, and in a few cases have built-in wooden sepulchral constructions square in shape; they were set on fire after the funeral, and a mound raised over the smouldering ruins.

Fig. 10   Sauromatian shaft-graves of various types (after Smirnov and Petrenko)

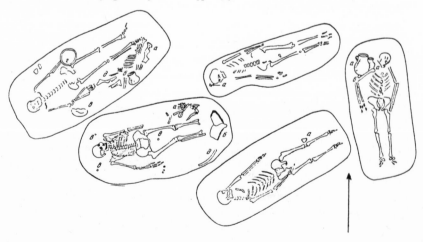

Corpses generally lay supine, but in the early stages of the culture a crouched position, typical of the Bronze Age, was not unusual. The heads for the most part faced the west or south-west. Cremation, entire or partial, was often effected on the spot, mainly in the Samara-Ural group, and fire seems to have been an essential part of the burial ritual. Traces of large hearths close to the shaft were found in most graves; sometimes the fire was lit over the shaft, and the floor of the grave was strewn with charcoal and ashes. The corpse was sometimes sprinkled with realgar (ochre), chalk or sulphur, or lumps of these substances were thrown into the grave shaft.

Most of the graves are poorly furnished and many have no equipment at all, but a good example of a richly furnished princely burial is that in the 'Sazonkin Bugor' barrow grave near Chernyi Yar on the lower Volga south-east of Volgograd. Several gold ornaments probably made in Pontic Greek colonies, an Olbian mirror, Baltic amber, weapons, etc. were found there.[2]

Plate 6

The usual Sauromatian grave goods consisted of weapons, small tools, personal ornaments and objects serving some special purpose, e.g. food, mostly in vessels. In the Samara-Ural group parts of horse-harness were sometimes found; they also appear in the fifth century BC in the Blumenfeld burials on the lower Volga —evidently in consequence of the arrival in the region of some tribal units from the southern Urals.

The main weapon was the bow, though no examples have actually been found; but arrow-heads are common, anything from one to three hundred being found in a single grave. They were mostly of bronze, occasionally of iron or bone; socketed, three-coned or three-edged, and sometimes double-edged. They vary widely in shape, several different types being found in a single burial, presumably used for different purposes. In the fifth century BC a new type of three-edged, tanged iron arrow-head appears in graves in the southern Urals region, later spreading to other areas of the culture. They were evidently introduced from

Central Asia where this type is common at an earlier date. The arrow-heads often lie loose, but are usually in leather or birch-bark quivers with their points downwards when found in any number. The quivers sometimes carry a bronze plate decorated with a zoomorphic ornament, and an iron hook designed to be fixed to the belt at the left side.

Fig. 11   A few iron swords, or daggers, usually with a bronze grip, worn on the right side, are found. Swords were much more important to the Sauromatians than to the Scythians, and in the fourth century BC they appear in many graves of the rank-and-file Sarmatians; they are mainly of the *akinakes* type of Western Asiatic origin. The early swords, mainly in the Lower Volga group, are very similar to, but longer (up to 130 cm.) than the swords of the Kuban and North Pontic branches of the Scythian culture. Later new varieties developed with a different pommel, grip and guard. Some pommels are in the shape of a square or oval bar, whereas others are of the zoomorphic 'antennae' type. The guards are either 'butterfly' or 'heart-shaped'. Daggers and swords of similar types are widespread in the Siberian steppe as far as the Yenissey, and in Soviet Central Asia. They were even adopted by some peoples of the forest zone.

Fig. 12   Iron lance-heads are seldom found, and the few bronze battle-axes are either of Siberian (Minusinsk) or Ananino (middle Volga-Kama) origin. To the category of talismans belong 'whetstones' perforated for fixing to the belt, which bear no traces of honing, and boar tusks carved with figures of rapacious animals or birds of prey, which are often affixed to quivers or sword straps.

Fig. 13   The pottery found in graves falls into two main categories, with some regional differences. One category consists of rough
Plate 7   thick-walled, flat-based pots developed from similar vessels typical of the preceding Bronze Age cultures. The second category, peculiar to the Volga group, consists of well-made, polished black ware, similar to that of the early Scythian culture

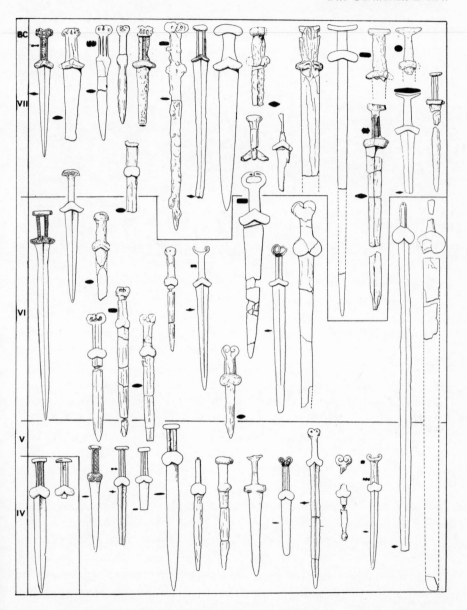

Fig. 11   Sauromatian swords of the seventh-fourth centuries BC (after Smirnov and Petrenko)

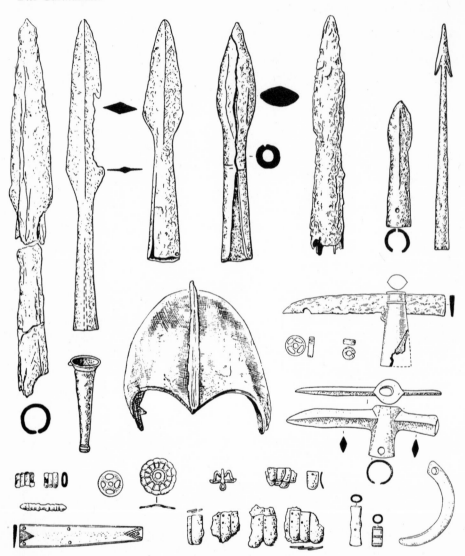

Fig. 12 Sauromatian military equipment of the sixth-fourth centuries BC (after Smirnov and Petrenko)

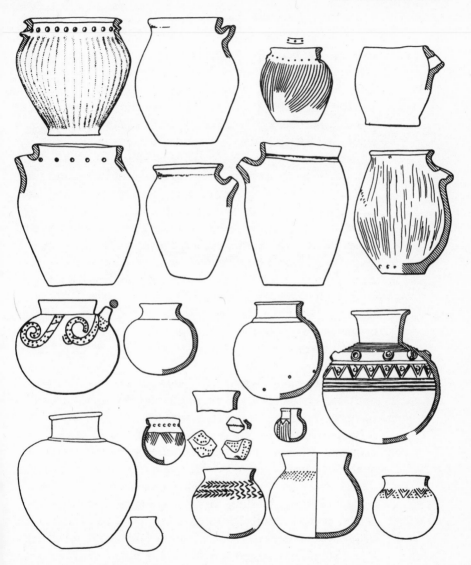

Fig. 13   Examples of Sauromatian pottery, characteristic of the Lower Volga (top) and Samara-Ural groups (after Smirnov)

of the Ukraine and the north-west Caucasus. It evidently originated in the west, and some vessels were apparently imported from the region of the Don delta.

From the second half of the fifth century BC a new type of round-bottomed, pear-shaped vessel is found in the southern Ural region. While showing no links with the local pottery of the preceding period, the vases are very similar to those that characterize the Sacian culture of south Kazakhstan and ancient Chorasmia on the lower Amu-Daria. They must have been introduced by newcomers to the territory, and later found their way to the lower Volga region, becoming typical of the Early Sarmatian culture in the subsequent period.

Fig. 14

Several cast bronze cauldrons were found either in graves or as isolated finds. Some have a rounded base but more typical are large specimens on a hollow stand, classified as of the 'Sarmatian' type. They usually contained the bones of sheep, occasionally those of horses and still more rarely of cattle. Characteristic of the Sauromatians were sheep carcasses either cut in two or dismembered (but always beheaded), found in richly furnished graves; in some burials there were three, or even more, entire headless sheep carcasses.

Characteristic of female burials are broken saddle querns, toilet utensils and personal ornaments: bronze, sometimes gold, bracelets, adornments for the temples and ear-rings, small decorated plates (with a zoomorphic ornament) sewn on to garments, pendants and amulets. Of interest is a fifth century BC

Fig. 15

figure of a bear sculptured in relief on a plaque made of elk antler. There are beads (loose or forming necklaces) made of gold, coloured glass, chalcedony, or other stones, and occasionally of amber. Bronze handled mirrors, a few of Olbian origin, are frequently found. Several richly furnished graves, exclusive to the Samara-Ural group, presumably those of priestesses, yielded the stone dishes thought to have been portable altars. Most of them are pedestalled (with three or four legs), all have raised edges, and

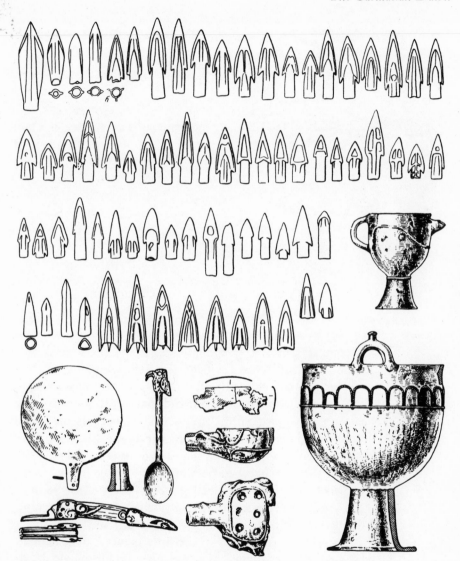

Fig. 14 Grave goods from the early-fifth-century BC barrow at Sobolevskaya near Buzuluk (Samara-Ural group) (after Smirnov)

47

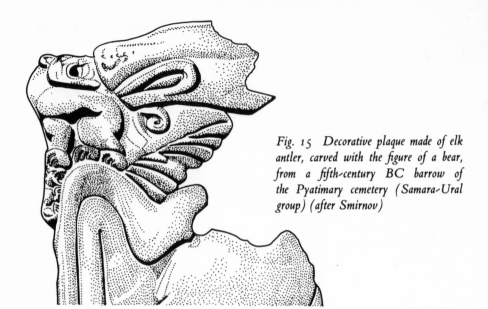

Fig. 15   Decorative plaque made of elk antler, carved with the figure of a bear, from a fifth-century BC barrow of the Pyatimary cemetery (Samara-Ural group) (after Smirnov)

some are decorated in the Scythian style. Traces of burning, possibly of incense, were noticed on them. Occasionally there are small glass vases or phials, imported from some West Asiatic centre and small spoons of bone or antler, with a carved zoo-morphic terminal on the handle. Though chiefly an attribute of male burials, weapons are also found in up to 20 per cent of the female graves investigated. In almost all the graves (male and female) iron knives are found; female graves contain iron or bone awls, while sheep astragali are found in those of several children.

Horse skeletons occur in both male and female (though more often in male) richly furnished princely graves of the Samara-Ural group (e.g. the cemetery of Pyatimary I near Orenburg), although sometimes, instead of a horse, bits and cheek-pieces had to act as a substitute. In the early graves bronze or bone cheek-pieces with three holes and zoomorphic terminals are found, but late in the sixth century BC a new type of iron bit and cheek-piece, probably of eastern origin, was introduced; this had

Fig. 16

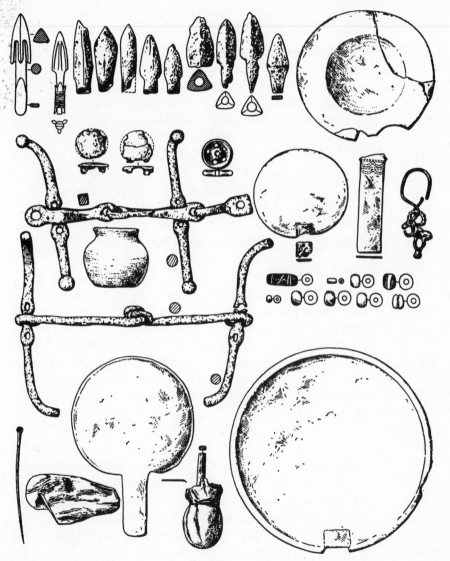

Fig. 16   Part of the equipment of barrow seven at Sara near Orsk, c. 500 BC (Samara-Ural group) (after Smirnov)

only two holes, and the terminals of some were in the shape of a griffin's or a horse's head. Bridles and straps are adorned with bronze plates sometimes decorated in the animal style. An early-fourth-century BC grave at Ak-Bulak (south of Orenburg) contained nine sets of horse harness. The Sarmatian saddles were probably similar to those of the Scythians, or the Altai people, having leather straps in place of wooden or iron stirrups. Finally, a very characteristic feature of the Samara-Ural group are halved boar tusks, or their bone imitations, with a carved or incised zoomorphic ornament. They evidently served as talismans or amulets, being found fastened either to the grip of a sword or to a bridle.

Plate 8

Human sacrifices, except of wives following their dead husbands, were restricted to the princely burials.

Sauromatian Origins

As we have already noted, the Bronze Age Srubnaya culture was evidently ancestral to the Volga branch of the Sauromatian culture, whereas the basic formative elements of the Samara-Ural group were the Ural and west Kazakhstan groups of the Andro-novo culture. The differences between these two parental cultures were to some extent evened out by the end of the Bronze Age by movements of each into the others' areas. Nevertheless, some scholars consider the two groups to be the archaeological equiva-lent of distinct peoples, although closely related to each other.

The transformation of the Srubnaya-Andronovo cultural complex into the Sauromatian culture took about two centuries. It was initiated by a north Caucasian, pre-Scythian current in the eighth and seventh centuries BC, as is attested by the presence of bronze objects, weapons, ornaments and parts of horse harness of the Koban and Novocherkassk type[3] found in several points in the areas of both groups.

Most probably the decisive influence in the formation of the Lower Volga group came from the north-west Caucasian group of the Scythian culture in the early sixth century BC, and, at a slightly later date, from its newly formed Lower Don group. Similarities between the early finds relating to the Sauromatians of the Lower Volga group and those of the North Pontic Scythian culture imply that the ancient links between the two branches of the Srubnaya descendants were still strong. This is further attested by the participation of the Sauromatians in the Scythian war against Darius in 514 BC, as recorded by Herodotus (IV, 119–123). These western contacts undoubtedly increased the differences already existing between the two main Sauromatian branches.

The events leading to the formation of the other, SamaraUral, branch were more complex and occurred at a somewhat later date. The North Caucasian (Koban) current which reached the Urals in the eighth century BC, was probably too weak to make any appreciable impression. A stronger influence will have been that of the North Pontic Scythian culture, although the territories of both lay nearly 500 miles apart. However, both countries were connected by the ancient trade route described by Herodotus by which the trade of the Scythians and Olbian Greeks reached the Urals and Siberia. The route must have crossed the territory of the SamaraUral group, carrying gold and other valuable goods, perhaps including furs; the North Pontic Scythian influence undoubtedly spread eastwards by this channel.

Another agency in the formation of this group was the splendid Achaemenid civilization. In the midsixth century BC Cyrus the Great pushed the frontiers of the Persian Empire deep into Central Asia, as far as the Sea of Aral. This conquest, which included Chorasmia, brought the nomads of the steppes north of the SyrDaria, and those of Kazakhstan, into more or less close contact with the Achaemenid civilization, exposing them to its influence.

The difference between the two branches of the Sauromatian culture were not initially of importance, being chiefly confined to a few specific features. But later, especially by the end of the fifth century BC, the differences increased considerably, when Central Asiatic, or West Siberian, elements appear in the re-mains of the Samara-Ural group, the Lower Volga group being affected to only a minor degree.

Sauromatian Trade

Although the wide variety of specific Sauromatian types of weapon, equipment and personal ornament implies the existence of a distinct class of master-smiths and founders, no remains of work-shops or foundries have so far been found, to compare with those uncovered on the Dnieper in ancient Scythia (see Chapter III). Men engaged in trade must have formed another social class, since numerous objects were imported and exported, mainly for the benefit of the Sauromatian aristocracy, as is sug-gested by the relatively large number of objects of foreign origin found in their graves.

The Sauromatians maintained connections with various countries, but there is a marked difference in this respect between the two branches of the people. The archaeological remains of the Lower Volga group indicate that they had close relations, mainly during the sixth and early fifth centuries BC, with the Scythians on the lower Don and in the Don delta and especially with those of the north-west Caucasus. That relations commenced at an early stage in the formation of the Lower Volga branch is proved by a Caucasian bronze helmet found on the Volga, and by the adoption by the Sauromatians of the short sword, or dagger, of the *akinakes* type characteristic of the early Scythians and the Medes in Iran. The polished black pottery also came from the Don delta, and the Scythian decorative animal style and the carnelian beads were probably of Caucasian, or Transcaucasian origin, all of which objects were adapted by Sauromatian master-craftsmen to meet local taste and needs. Only a few objects of eastern origin, however, were found in the Lower Volga group.

Trade was carried on between the Samara-Ural group, especially its western division, and the Scythians in the Ukraine. Several objects imported from the West are found in the Samara-Ural area: Olbian bronze mirrors, two specimens of which were decorated with feline figures (the easternmost of these found at Bish-Oba near Orsk); cheek-pieces; ear-rings and ornaments for the temples; small decorative objects and a few other items, all exclusively of the sixth and early fifth centuries BC.

The relations of this group with countries to the east, especially those of Central Asia, are revealed by a series of objects, found chiefly in graves around Orsk; all are of a slightly later date than the western imported goods. Among them are daggers of the Kazakhstan or Central Asiatic type, Achaemenid silver and bronze plates, and eastern-type flat bronze mirrors, all of the fifth century BC. The 'Scythian' decorative style of a Siberian character was among the eastern features adopted by the Sauromatians of this group.

CONDITIONS IN CENTRAL ASIA: THE EARLY NOMADS

The Sauromatians and Scythians were the westernmost peoples of the large complex of Iranian speaking nomads, who in the sixth and fifth centuries BC lived in the steppes of modern Kazakhstan and Central Asia. In course of time they were forced to move mainly westwards, and may subsequently have crossed into Europe. The history of these nomads, especially those of the northern Asiatic steppe, must therefore be considered as an integral part of the Sarmatian past.

The name 'Scythians', or 'Eastern Scythians', was often applied to the peoples of the Kazakhstan steppes; those further south, in the steppes of Central Asia, were mostly called 'Sacians', the Persian equivalent of 'Scythians'. Light is thrown on a number of the Sacian peoples by the writings of Herodotus and Persian records, by sculptures in relief in Persian palaces, and by rock carvings commemorating Persian victories. A number of their tribal names are also recorded. However, the position regarding their kindred tribes further north, in the steppes of modern Kazakhstan, is rather different. A few names of the tribes on the eastern border of this complex are to be found in Chinese records, but the most important, and also the earliest source is the report of the journey undertaken by Aristeas of Proconnesus about the middle of the seventh century BC. This journey is described by Herodotus (IV, 13–15), who also adds information obtained (during his stay in the north Pontic city of Olbia) from Greek merchants trading with these remote peoples.

Aristeas' report has been discussed by many scholars,[4] who differ in their reconstructions of his route and their location of the countries and peoples he mentions. Most scholars agree, however, that he must have crossed the Urals and that some of the peoples he met were Iranian-speaking nomads, evidently the ancestors of the Sarmatian-Alan tribes who later entered the North Pontic area. At that time they must have represented the Andronovo culture.

Archaeological work in the vast steppe country of Kazakhstan has been very sporadic and large areas of the country remain uninvestigated. Furthermore, many graves have proved to have been ransacked either in antiquity or, more often, by Russian treasure-seekers of the eighteenth and nineteenth centuries. A few
Plate 9
of the spoils have found their way to museums, and the largest and most splendid of these is Peter the Great's famous collection of Siberian gold objects in the 'Scythian' style, now in the Hermitage Museum at Leningrad.

Several distinct groups of archaeological remains from the late sixth and fifth centuries BC have been found, and these are evidently to be associated with a number of separate peoples whose names we do not know but who are jointly referred to in Soviet literature as 'Early Nomads'. Identification of some of them with the peoples mentioned by Aristeas—although more or less well-founded—will always be conjectural. Nor are the names of the steppe peoples who successively appeared in the North Pontic area much of a guide since the nomadic peoples, represented by the established groups of archaeological remains in Kazakhstan, must have been split up during their forced retreat. Once arrived in Europe, the emergent elements most probably consisted of entirely re-formed units, and were presumably known by the name of the strongest tribe in the new formation. The hetero-geneous character of the Sauromatians, to which attention has already been drawn, is even more marked in the Sarmatian-Alan tribes at the time of their stay in Europe.

The culture of the Early Nomads of the sixth and fifth centuries BC differed in several respects from that of the North Pontic Scythians, but also—to a lesser degree—from that of the Sauro-matians. Their similarities and common traits, especially in the field of their 'Scythian' art, are due to their common roots, the most important being the strong impact upon them of the Persian offspring of the ancient oriental civilization, which was the chief factor in the formation of both.

The 'Early Nomad' peoples have seldom been taken into account in discussions of the Sarmatian past. Here, we shall devote some attention to them. We possess no detailed description of these peoples but the report by Herodotus on the kindred Massagetae of Central Asia (I, 201–206) may give some insight into the mode of life and customs of the steppe tribes further north.

THE MASSAGETAE

The Massagetae, the mightiest Sacian folk of the Achaemenid period in Central Asia, held the territory between the Rivers Amu-Daria and Syr-Daria east of the Sea of Aral, north of ancient Chorasmia. Their centre lay in the former delta of the Syr-Daria, now no longer in existence. The country was well watered during the first millennium BC, and was densely populated. Eastwards it extended nearly 450 km. deep into the area which is now either desert or semi-desert.

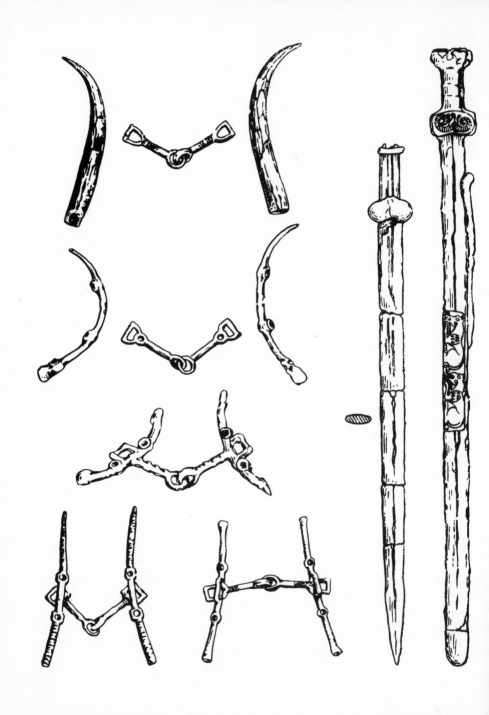

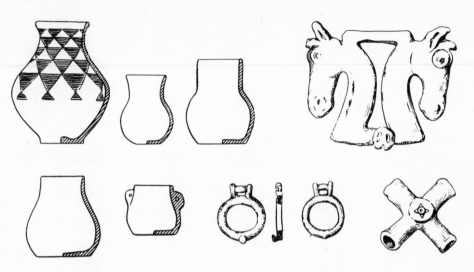

Fig. 17   Horse harness, swords and pottery from Massagetan~Sacian burials of the sixth~fifth centuries BC at Tagisken and Uygarak on the lower Syr~Daria (after Tolstov and Itina)

According to Herodotus, the Massagetae were nomads who 'resemble the Scythians in their dress and mode of life'. Their name derives from an Iranian word meaning 'the fish',[5] and both Herodotus and Strabo emphasize that they were fish~eaters. They drank milk, and their children lived in wagons drawn by oxen. Strabo distinguishes among them several tribes: 'Some of them inhabit mountains, some plains, others marshes formed by the rivers, and others the islands in the marshes. But the country is inundated most of all by the River Araxes (Syr~Daria), which splits into numerous branches and empties by its other branch into the other sea in the north . . .' Those who lived in the delta were breeders of cattle, horses and camels, and they also cultivated irrigated plots. Handicrafts were well developed. The inhabitants of the plains, although possessing land, did not till it but lived on sheep and fish in the nomadic fashion.

The Massagetae were warlike and fought both on foot and on horseback, and 'are said to be both powerful and valiant'. Their weapons were bows, javelins and battle~axes, which were still

Fig. 17

made of bronze, as no iron was found in the country, 'but copper and gold were abundant'. Their 'heads, belts and shoulder pieces' were decorated with gold; they 'put bronze breast-plates on the chests of horses', and their bridle-bits and cheek-pieces were also embellished with gold. The famous gold plates of the so-called Oxus (Amu-Daria) treasure acquaint us with their dress; and their kindred the Amyrgian Sacae, who lived in the steppe east of the Caspian Sea, wore similar clothes, with the exception of their caps which came to a point and 'stood erect'.

Fig. 18

Plates 1, 2

Plate 3

Originally the social organization of the Massagetae seems to have been matriarchal, and Herodotus remarks that they 'use women promiscuously'. They worshipped the sun, to which they sacrificed horses, but Zoroastrianism must also have been wide-spread among them and the kindred tribes of the Central Asiatic and Kazakhstan steppes. Herodotus also describes a strange custom which implies that they practised a ritual cannibalism: 'When a man has attained a great age, all his kinsmen meet, and sacrifice him, together with cattle of several kinds: and when they have boiled the flesh, they feed on it.' A similar practice has been recorded amongst the Derbices, who lived somewhere near the present Irano-Afghan frontier, and also among the Issedonians. Corroborative evidence is provided by the discovery in some Sauromatian barrow graves in the Southern Urals of pieces of human bones in the remains of funeral feasts, along with those of animals. This strange custom seems to have been inherited by all these tribes from their common Andronovo ancestors in the Bronze Age.

The culture of all the Massagetan tribes was affected by that of Chorasmia.[6] Characteristic of the southern region are 'mausolea', burial-places of the local ruling class, built of sun-baked bricks, circular in plan and divided into four grave-chambers. These were adopted from Chorasmia and contained richly furnished burials consisting chiefly of cremations, although for the most part they had been looted in antiquity. More common are burials under

Fig. 18 Gold personal ornaments decorated in the animal style, from barrows at Tagisken in Soviet central Asia (after Tolstov and Itina)

mounds, either in shafts or on the original surface; while some very poorly furnished graves, including a few with no goods at all, were evidently those of rank-and-file Sacians, or the former population which they had subdued.

In barrow graves investigated at Uygarak the corpses lay diagonally with the head to the east, in square burial chambers. Similar 'diagonal' graves found in the southern Urals are of later date, and later still, in the second century BC, they became characteristic of the lower Volga area, where they have been attributed to the Roxolani. Those in the Syr-Daria delta are the earliest of all burials of this type. The grave goods consist mainly of pottery and bronze arrow-heads of the Scythian type; in some richly furnished graves gold leaf, pieces of horse harness decorated in the Scythian animal style and, in one instance an iron sword, were found. The bits have stirrup-shaped terminals.

Fig. 19

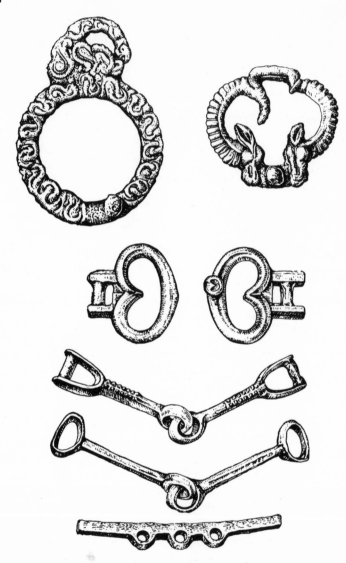

Fig. 19 Parts of bronze horse harness from three barrows at Uygarak on the lower Syr-Daria (after Tolstov)

During the Achaemenid period, the Massagetae maintained close relations with the eastern branch of the Sauromatians, and the nomad tribes of the steppe-country to the north. These peoples adopted many elements of the Chorasmian and Massagetan culture, especially the portable stone 'altars', earlier associated with Central Asia. The sepulchral constructions excavated in several mounds, such as shafts with a niche, 'catacombs', or mounds built of stone, are new to the Ural steppe, but have been recorded in Central Asia in the preceding period. Several objects found in the Sauromatian graves dating from the second half of the fifth century BC either were imported from Chorasmia or the country of the Massagetae, or must have passed through them as intermediaries. Among them was wheel-turned pottery of a Central Asiatic type, and most important, many Achaemenid goods such as beads of alabaster and sardonyx, *Cyprea moneta* shells, Iranian silver and bronze bowls, the latter being found in Early Sarmatian graves (post-Sauromatian) and also in those of the Kama region further to the north.

PEOPLES ENCOUNTERED BY ARISTEAS: 'OTHER SCYTHIANS'

No 'Scythian' objects found east of the Urals, those of the fine Peter the Great Collection in the Leningrad Hermitage[7] not excepted, are of a date prior to the late sixth century BC. At the time of Aristeas' journey, which was undertaken not later than the middle of the seventh century BC, the 'Scythian' culture had not yet come into being, and the peoples mentioned in his account whether in Europe or Asia, must have been those of the final stage of the Srubnaya culture in Europe and of the Andronovo and Karasuk cultures in Asia. There is no archaeological evidence of any sizeable tribal movements in that area during the later part of the seventh and the sixth centuries BC, before the gradual transformation of these cultures into those of a Scythian type.

Aristeas' journey started at the mouth of the Don, and he must then have travelled along the Volga, across the territory of Herodotus' 'Sauromatians', following the well-established north Caucasian trade route. On leaving this, he entered first the country of the Budini, then the country of the Thyssagetae—probably on the middle Volga. Afterwards, he seems to have crossed the Ural Mountains along the valley of one of the tributaries of the Kama.

Among the peoples whom Aristeas encountered were the Ircae, who lived in 'a thickly wooded country', evidently the forest zone on the eastern side of the Urals, and were related to the Thyssagetae. They rode horses, and when hunting laid ambushes by climbing trees. This description suggests a domicile somewhere around modern Cheliabinsk and in parts of the southern Urals. Archaeologically, they can be equated with a branch of the Andronovo culture which seized that area during the Late Bronze Age, evolving into the Cheliabinsk group, a hybrid of the genuine Sauromatian culture, in the late-sixth century BC.[8]

Aristeas next mentions the 'other Scythians' who 'rebelled against the Royal Scythians, and so came to this country.' Their country is described as 'level and deep-soiled'. It was probably the black-earth area east of the river Tobol up to the Irtysh and beyond, including modern north Kazakhstan. Whilst finds of a Scythian character bear out the existence of the 'other Scythians', at the time of Aristeas these presumably belonged to the local Andronovo branch, who are believed to have originally inhabited the steppe to the south and south-east, in central Kazakhstan, which the Issedonians seized towards the end of the second millennium BC.

Modern northern Kazakhstan, a vast area extending for about 800 km., within which in the sixth–fifth centuries BC the anonymous tribes of the 'other Scythians' lived, has been insufficiently investigated.[9] The barrow graves consist of earthen mounds, showing a tolerable degree of uniformity both in their

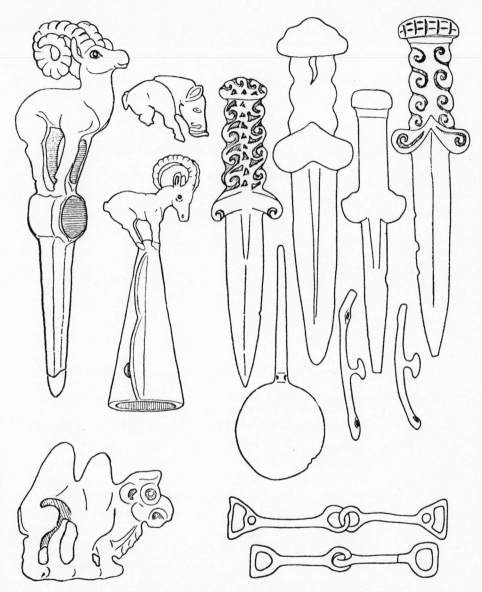

Fig. 20   Daggers, horse harness and ornaments in the animal style of the 'Early Nomads' found in North Kazakhstan, fifth-fourth centuries BC (after Arslanova)

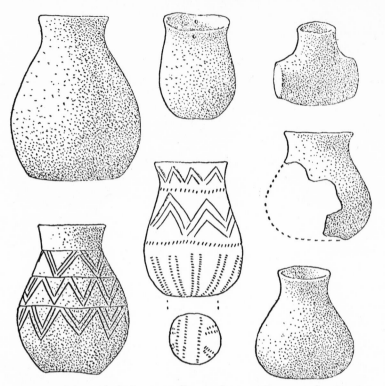

construction and their generally modest equipment, despite the several hundred kilometres separating the sites. Many similarities link those in the west of the country with the graves of the Samara‑Ural group of the Sauromatian culture.

The burials are in oval shafts lined with timber logs or, occasionally, stone slabs. The bodies were inhumed supine with their heads to the west, but there were also instances of cremation. The few unpillaged graves that have been found were furnished rather poorly, and many had no equipment or yielded only a few objects, mainly three‑edged 'Scythian' bronze arrow‑heads, very occasionally a short iron sword or dagger of the *akinakes* type, a round bronze mirror with a loop, occasionally an oval stone plate with raised edges, beads of glossy paste, sometimes one or two clay vessels, and a small iron knife near the bones of a sheep's leg.

Fig. 20

Fig. 21

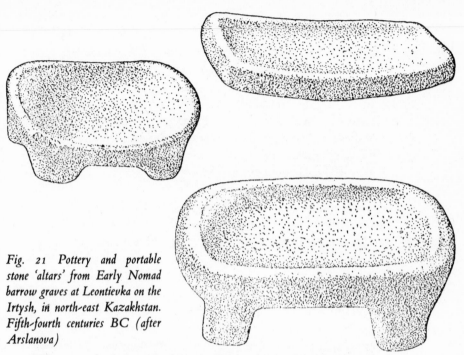

Fig. 21 Pottery and portable stone 'altars' from Early Nomad barrow graves at Leontievka on the Irtysh, in north-east Kazakhstan. Fifth-fourth centuries BC (after Arslanova)

Who were the 'other Scythians'? With which of the Sarmatian peoples who later appeared in Europe may they be linked? The questions cannot be answered yet; perhaps these tribes never attained any pre-eminence and were simply embodied into one, or more, of the successive Sarmatian waves retreating westwards.

The Issedonians

The most remote of the Early Nomad, proto-Sarmatian people visited by Aristeas appear to have been the Issedonians. Their territory, it would seem, extended over the whole central Kazakhstan plateau and the Melkosopochnik Mountains, from the region of the town of Djezkazgan, about 450 km. south-west of Karaganda, eastwards up to the Irtysh River somewhere north of Semipalatinsk, over a distance of more than 1000 km.

The geographical position of the area, and its archaeological material which is attributable to the Issedonians, suggests that the latter may be identified with the proto-Asi-Iasi-Aorsi, at least with that section of the people who by the end of the fifth century BC had moved westwards and entered Sauromatian territory. Some Soviet authors place the Issedonians in the Semirechie region east of Lake Balkhash, identifying them with the Wu-sun (called the Usuny in Russian archaeological literature) who later migrated southwards into the eastern part of Soviet Central Asia. However, placing them in Semirechie conflicts with Herodotus' account (I, 201; IV, 13, 16, 25–27).

Herodotus says that the women of the Issedonians 'have equal authority with the men' which, again, seems to be a survival of their former matriarchy. He refers, moreover, to the strange practice of ritual cannibalism, also recorded among the Massa-getae.

The barrow graves, investigated at various points in central Kazakhstan, differ in both size and construction.[10] Five chrono-logical groups covering the time from the sixth century BC to approximately AD 500 have been distinguished. The dates of these periods more or less correspond to those associated with the development of the Sarmatian peoples in the Volga steppe and southern Urals.

The barrow graves of the earliest period in the northern region of the country are mainly earthen mounds, but in other sectors the most common type consists of small or medium-sized mounds of stones. They usually form small cemeteries, that at Supra-Oba consisting of fifteen mounds. The grave-shafts, whether in earthen or stone mounds, are oval, narrow, often lined and covered with stone slabs, or with logs. Shafts with a niche ('catacombs') have also been discovered, the earliest of the Scytho-Sarmatian complex. Almost all the tombs had been pillaged and only a few objects from the original equipment were found. They were similar to those from graves in north

Kazakhstan: bronze bits with stirrup-shaped terminals, bronze arrow-heads, flat bronze mirrors, a few gold ear-rings and small decorated gold plates or some other gold ornament. One or two clay vessels were found, some, especially those from the earliest barrow graves (Dyndy-Bay), recalling the pre-Scythian pottery of the area and exhibiting features of the Andronovo and Karasuk cultures.

Very characteristic of the 'Early Nomads', or, as they are sometimes called, the 'Saco-Scythians', are large stone mounds to which two low elliptical stone walls were joined on their eastern side, about 20 to 500 m. long, and occasionally enclosing an area up to 150 m. wide. Small stone cairns terminated both walls. A popular name, 'barrow graves with whiskers', has been given to these structures. They were evidently the tombs of outstanding members of the local aristocracy. The custom developed during the transitional period from the Andronovo to the 'Saco-Scythian' culture and lasted down to the fourth century BC. No unpillaged barrow of this type has been found. The burials were in oval shafts, as in the small mounds, and their equipment was similar to that in the graves of the rank-and-file Issedonians; they might, however, have been furnished with several gold objects later looted by treasure-seekers.

Fig. 22

Traces of copper-mining have been found in the rich metallifer-ous regions, especially in the Karkaralinsk ridge, which has peaks from 1360 to 1560 m. above the sea level. Copper-mining had started there by the middle of the second millennium BC under the Andronovians, and the mines were still active during the Saco-Scythian period.

Fig. 23

According to Herodotus, the territory then inhabited by the Issedonians was not their original country, which they had been forced to abandon by the Arimaspians. This presumably lay further to the east, in the valley of the upper Irtysh, east and south-east of Semipalatinsk. The account corroborates the archaeological evidence, which indicates that the local Andro-

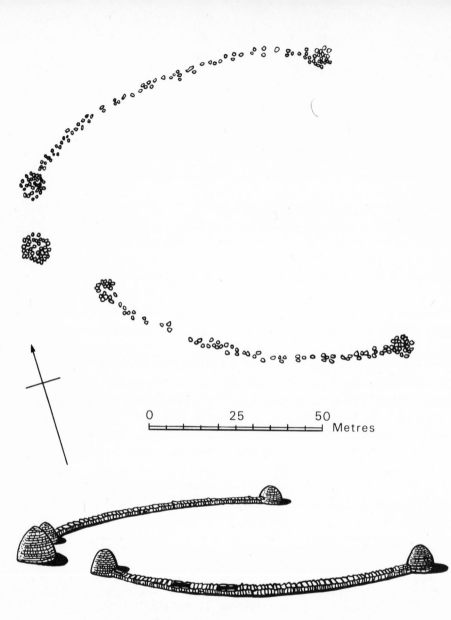

Fig. 22 Plan and reconstruction of a barrow 'with whiskers' at Dzhanaydar near Ulutay in the western part of central Kazakhstan (after Orazbaev)

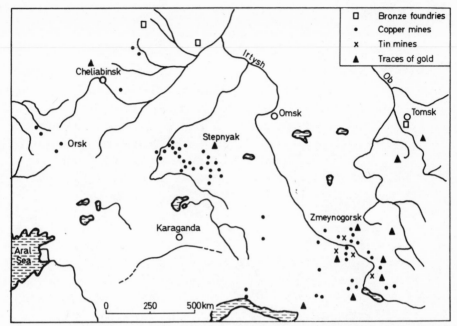

Fig. 23   Siberian mineral resources exploited in the Late Bronze Age and in the Early Nomad period. The mines were mostly abandoned in the fourth century BC (after Zolotova and Griaznov)

novo tribes had been displaced by an expansion of the Karasuk people by the end of the second millennium BC. In moving westwards, the Issedonians displaced another group of the Andronovians, the ancestors of the 'other Scythians' described in the preceding section.

The Argippaei

The Argippaei were a non-Iranian people who, according to Herodotus, lived 'at the foot of lofty mountains', and were neighbours of both the 'other Scythians' and the Issedonians. Reports that they were 'bald from birth' may have resulted from a misinterpretation of their custom of shaving the head. Herodotus writes of them that they 'are flat-nosed and have large chins', features characteristic of the Mongolian race; they 'speak a peculiar language', evidently a non-Iranian one, and they were probably of Ugrian-, or Turkic-speaking stock. He also emphasizes that they possessed no warlike weapons and were considered sacred by other peoples; 'the Scythians frequently go there (to the Argippaei) and transact business by means of seven interpreters and seven languages', and ample information on this people can be obtained from the Pontic Greeks.

The conclusion is that the Argippaei lived at the terminus of the great trade route of Herodotus' time. This ran from Olbia along the River Ingul and a short distance overland to the Dnieper somewhere near Cherkassy or Kremenchug; there it turned eastwards, following approximately the border of the steppe and forest-steppe, ultimately reaching the Altai Mountains in the centre of Asia. Herodotus does not mention what commodities were sought by the western traders, but we may guess that they were attracted by the mineral wealth of the country of the Argippaei, particularly gold. Presumably only gold would entice western merchants to travel well over 4000 km. and overcome considerable language difficulties. It has been suggested that the sacred immunity of the Argippaei may be compared with that enjoyed by tribes of African blacksmiths: the Argippaei may have been skilled miners, foundrymen and, above all, goldsmiths who worked for all the neighbouring peoples.

There are a few traces of western penetration in the Altai area. A Caucasian bronze helmet of the sixth century BC was found in the mountains, and bronze ornaments for the temples terminating in a disc, probably made locally but modelled on specimens typical of the Scythian culture of the sixth century in the Ukraine, were excavated in a series of graves in the valley of the upper Ob south of Barnaul and in the region of Biisk. It is difficult to ascertain what goods were bartered for gold, but the trade was obviously profitable to the western merchants.

The assumption that the Argippaei were miners places their country in the rich metalliferous region on the upper Irtysh east of Semipalatinsk, which includes the lower western ranges of the Altai in the north, and the Kalbinskii ridge in the south. Tin and copper mines of the period have been found in this area, and in Zmeynogorsk, about 150 km. north-east of Semipalatinsk, traces of ancient gold mines have been discovered.[11] Signs of gold mining have also been found at several points in the mountains along the upper Irtysh and its eastern tributaries. However, as this area has been insufficiently explored, it is not possible to attribute the archaeological remains definitely to the Argippaei. A few settlements and small 'flat' cemeteries examined further north, in the valley of the upper Ob south of Barnaul, and in the region of Biisk may, perhaps, be attributed to a northern branch of the people:[12] the Mongoloid character of the cranial material is also consistent with Herodotus' description. The culture associated with these archaeological remains is known as the Bolsherechenskaya culture, and is considered to represent a further development of the local branch of the Karasuk culture. However, no copper or other metals were available in the area, except in its southernmost parts, although remains of a bronze foundry were discovered in a settlement on the River Ob south of Barnaul.

The Arimaspians

Herodotus writes that 'our knowledge respecting the country and the nations in front of [the Argippaei and Issedonians] is very good' but beyond the Argippaei 'no one can speak with certainty, for lofty and impassable mountains form their boundary, and no one has ever crossed them'; the Argippaei say 'that men with goats' feet inhabit these mountains'. Another legendary people who lived in that area 'beyond' or 'above' the Argippaei and the Issedonians, 'are the men with only one eye' whom the 'Scythians call the Arimaspians', and who 'continually encroached upon their neighbours'. Relations between Arimaspians and Issedonians were uneasy, a state of affairs which implies that they must have been neighbours. The Arimaspians had expelled the Issedonians and seized their original country.

At the time of Aristeas, the Arimaspian country probably extended east and south-east of Semipalatinsk and must have been partially identical with that of the Argippaei. The story of its seizure and the expulsion of the Issedonians calls to mind the expansion of the Karasuk culture into that very area late in the second millennium BC, when the inhabitants were a local branch of the Andronovians, presumably the ancestors of the Issedonians. Some were overrun by the newcomers and absorbed by them, but the majority must have retreated westwards, setting in motion other groups of their kindred Andronovians, among them the ancestors of the 'other Scythians'.

Finds of the Maiemirskaya culture[13] dating from the sixth and fifth centuries BC in the valley of the upper Ob and upper Irtysh, and the surrounding lower ranges and foothills of the Altai, may be attributed to the Arimaspians. No settlements, merely graves under mounds built of stones mixed with earth, and a series of isolated objects, have been found. A find from Zmeyno-gorsk, a bronze outfit of a mounted warrior and his horse, deserves special mention, as does a fine decorated bronze dagger; both were found in the gold-bearing region.

In the Ob valley, the Maiemirskaya finds overlap with those of the Bolsherechenskaya culture. Excavation of a large barrow-grave cemetery at Berezovka near Biisk, comprising over 120 mounds, has revealed that it was coeval with the remains of the Bolsherechenskaya culture of the same area. The people buried in mounds did not belong to the latter culture although they lived in the same country. The two cultures are virtually identical materially, but the cranial material reveals that the people of the Bolsherechenskaya culture were of the Mongoloid racial type whereas those buried in mounds were of the Europoid type with only a slight Mongoloid admixture. Those buried in the Maiemir-skaya mounds were evidently members of the ruling class and

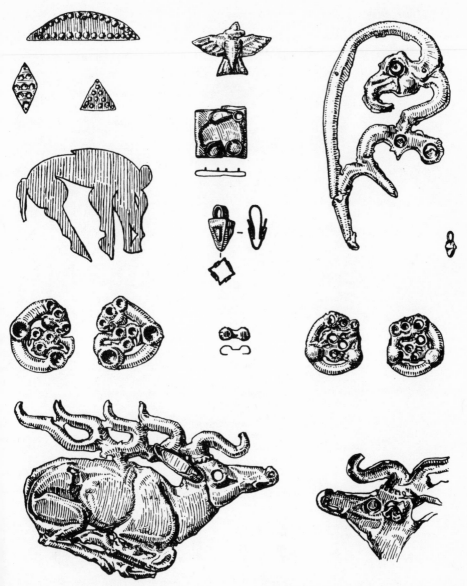

Fig. 24 Gold ornaments from barrow grave 5 in the Chiliktinskaya valley, East Kazakhstan. Carbon 14 tests give a date of 430–250 BC (after Chernikov)

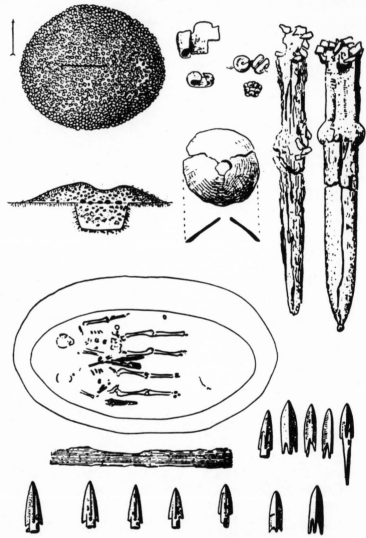

Fig. 25   *Plan and section of barrow grave 25 at Kzylauz in the valley of the Ili in East Kazakhstan, and its grave goods. c. 500 BC (after Akishev and Kushaev)*

may be identified with the Arimaspians. Their relations with the people of the Bolsherechenskaya culture, presumably a branch of the Argippaei, are not clear but the latter may have been under the protection of the Arimaspians.

Barrow graves of the 'Early Nomads' investigated further south in eastern Kazakhstan, in the valley of the upper Irtysh, may also be attributed to the Arimaspians. Among these are mounds excavated on the northern slopes of the Tarbagatay ridge, about 350 km. south-east of Semipalatinsk, dating mainly from the late fifth and fourth centuries BC, slightly later than those described above. They have been incorrectly attributed to the Issedonians.[14]

The most spectacular of the group was the Chiliktinskii barrow grave No. 5, containing a double burial. Although it had been ransacked, 524 gold objects, weighing more than 100 grams, were discovered in addition to a fragment of an iron object and thirteen double-edged socketed bronze arrow-heads in a leather (or hide) quiver decorated with fourteen thin gold plates in the shape of 'Scythian' stags. The date of this tomb has been put at the turn of the seventh and sixth centuries BC, but its radiocarbon dating is 340 ± 90 BC (LE-247), that is 430–250 BC.

Fig. 24

The Scythian animal style, in which several of the objects mentioned above are decorated, is related to that of the Tagarskaya culture of the Minusinsk valley. However, the construction of the mounds investigated in eastern Kazakhstan links them with the Pazyryk group of barrow graves in the Altai highland on the one hand, and, on the other, with Sacian burial mounds further south, in the ancient countries of Sogdiana and Bactria in the Tien-Shan and Pamir Mountains. These southern connections pose a problem about the identity of the people of the East Kazakhstan mounds, the presumed Arimaspians. Some scholars connect the Arimaspians' name with that of the Arians, which would imply an Iranian origin; others maintain that they were of Turcoman stock, possibly with some Iranian ad-

Fig. 25

mixture. It seems possible, however, to identify them with the Wu-sun (Usuny) of the Chinese Chronicles, a Tocharian speaking people,[15] as this view seems to be supported by the fact that the founders of the Tagarskaya culture of the Minusinsk valley were presumably Tocharians. Later, they were forced to retreat southwards from east Kazakhstan, but some smaller units might have moved westwards and ultimately reached the steppes of Eastern Europe as a component of the Eastern Alans (Chapter V).

The Pazyryk Group

The 'gold-guarding griffins' or 'men with goats' feet', mentioned by Herodotus, who lived in the 'lofty and inaccessible' mountains of the High Altai, were possibly a branch of the Arimaspians, as their barrow graves were similar to those of east Kazakhstan. They are concentrated in the Altai highlands, some about 1600 m. above sea level (Pazyryk), or even up to 2000 m. (the Tuva region[16]). Much has been written in several languages on the Pazyryk mounds, in which frozen corpses, horses, and many perishable objects of wool, leather and other organic matter, including furs and carpets, have been found fairly well preserved. They afford a unique opportunity of studying the dress, equip-ment, art, taste and customs of the mounted pastoral nomads of the fifth century BC.

Characteristic of the Pazyryk group are large mounds con-taining richly furnished graves, evidently belonging to the local chiefs or members of the aristocracy. Immediately after the funeral, they were ransacked, and this reflects a deep social division in the Pazyryk society, presumably due to the subjection of the indigenous people, possibly a branch of the Argippaei, by a stronger invader. The Pazyryk graves are mostly of the fifth century BC. Radiocarbon tests show their dates to range from *c.* 500 BC (Tuekta; RUL-132) to *c.* 400 BC (Pazyryk II; RUL-120), which is conspicuously close to the Persian conquest of the

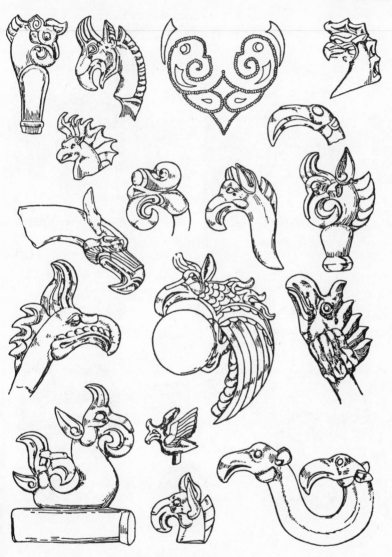

Fig. 26 Examples of representations of griffins in the art of the Pazyryk group
of the fifth-fourth centuries BC (after Rudenko)

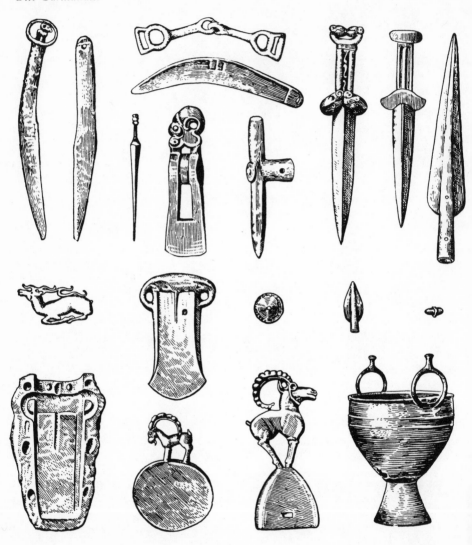

Fig. 27 Copper and bronze objects and a mould, characteristic of the Tagarskaya culture of southern Siberia (after Avdusin)

southern part of Soviet Central Asia. It seems therefore likely that some Iranian, or Tocharian, tribes in the conquered area migrated northwards along the Tien-Shan Mountains and ultimately settled in the High Altai. The people obviously kept up contacts with their kindred in the south, and it seems that Achaemenid influence reached the Altai in this way.[17] The intimate relations between the High Altai people (especially its rulers) and countries to the south-west are attested by objects imported from these regions, mostly luxuries (*e.g.* leopard skins). Their fine horses were evidently descended from the Central Asiatic or Iranian higher breeds. Achaemenid daggers of the *akinakes* type and other weapons were adopted by the peoples of the Tien-Shan Mountains and the Altai, and then by the Early Nomads of the Kazakhstan steppe country. Most of the decorative motifs characteristic of the Pazyryk 'Scythian' art—ibexes, griffins and other fantastic animals, scenes of combat, palmettes and the lotus motif—were evidently derived from Achaemenid art and they soon became typical of the 'Scythian' art of Siberia. The reference by Herodotus to the country of the 'gold-guarding griffins' possibly reflects a marked predilection for the griffin in the decorative art of the Altai.

Fig. 26

Gold seems to have been the main source of the Pazyryk chieftains' wealth, and it was probably the gold trade that was responsible for their maintenance of close relations with the south; the southern luxuries found in Pazyryk graves were possibly received in exchange for it. On the other hand, the importance of the gold trade poses a problem about the relations between the Pazyryk people and the Argippaei, whose territory partly overlapped; the Argippaei may have worked as miners and goldsmiths for the Pazyryk chieftains in return for their protection.

The Pazyryk community lasted for about two centuries, ceasing early in the third century BC. The disappearance of these accomplished people is difficult to explain, but it was probably due to their defeat by the mighty Massagetae, when they, or certainly their rulers, were presumably forced to leave their country for an unknown refuge.

The Tagarskaya Culture

Finally, some attention should be given to the Tagarskaya culture, the north-easternmost group of the 'Scythian' complex, although it differed considerably from the other groups.

This culture extended over the Minusinsk valley on the Yenissey, north-east of the Altai Mountains. Its people were settled farmers, though they supplemented agriculture by a nomadic pastoral way of life. They are mainly identified by *Fig. 27* graves (several richly furnished) and isolated objects, only a few settlements having been found. The culture had no roots in the country and no connection with the preceding Karasuk culture. It was presumably formed by newcomers from the south-west, from Tien-Shan, Fergana or another Central Asiatic country.[18]

There were evidently strong class divisions in this society, probably due to a conquest of the country, early in the fifth century BC, by mounted nomads from east Kazakhstan, who brought with them fine Central Asiatic horses and the Scythian animal style of decoration closely related to that of the Altai Pazyryk group. The newcomers appear to have been absorbed quickly, but nevertheless left their 'Scythian' imprint on the *Plate 10* Tagarskaya culture. The population was basically Europoid with a slight Mongoloid admixture, representing anthropological types peculiar to the local cultures of the Bronze Age. Most authors believe that they were of Indo-European stock; N. L. Chlenova points out that the ancient toponomy of the Minusinsk valley is Indo-European, most likely Tocharian, and the founders of the Tagarskaya culture may therefore have been a Tocharian branch of Indo-Europeans. Early in the third century BC they were forced to retreat westwards, and many probably joined the Alans in their withdrawal towards the Volga steppes.

CHAPTER III

The Early Sarmatian Period

Fourth and third centuries BC

DEVELOPMENTS IN ASIA

THE DECLINE IN Achaemenid power late in the fifth century BC enabled the Chorasmians to shake off Persian domination. The archaeological material from the end of the fifth and early fourth centuries BC indicates that tribal migrations must have taken place at that time in Central Asia and the steppes of Kazakhstan. It seems probable that the formation of a strong tribal union of the Massagetae, possibly with their close kin the Chorasmians, lay at the root of these disturbances.

The destruction by Alexander the Great of the Achaemenid monarchy and his subsequent conquest of Bactria and Sogdiana in 330–328 BC also influenced the history and development of all the peoples of Central Asia. Neither the Chorasmians nor the Massagetae were subjugated by Alexander, but as a result of having to fight against the highly trained and organized Macedonian army, they developed new military tactics using armoured cavalry, the 'cataphracti' (see Chapter I). Some authors think that the Massagetae owed their conquests solely to the use of this armoured cavalry against weaker adversaries.

In the fourth and third centuries BC, the Massagetae subdued nearly all the nomad tribes of Central Asia north of the Macedonian frontier, eastwards to the Tien-Shan Mountains, and possibly many tribes of the Kazakhstan steppes; this led to a tremendous extension of their culture which to a great extent derived from that of Achaemenid Iran. A strong Iranian influence is also reflected in the splendid gold jewellery found in some princely barrow graves in the steppe, which was now beginning to be set with coloured glass or semi-precious stones. The Turkic-speaking Huns, who roamed the steppe further to the east up to the Chinese border, had also to acknowledge Massagetan suzerainty for about a century. It was not until 165 BC that the Huns defeated the Massagetae and drove them southwards and westwards out of their lands.

The expansion of the Massagetae affected the neighbouring steppe-tribes. Central Asiatic types of graves and objects dating from the turn of the fifth century BC are found in the southern Ural region. The appearance in the fourth century in northern Kazakhstan of barrow graves ('kurgans') 'with whiskers', typical of the Issedonians of Central Kazakhstan, seems to reflect the withdrawal, under Massagetan pressure, of some Issedonian tribes, who—at least for a time—kept to their ancient culture in the new country.[1]

The might of the Massagetae was not destined to last for long. Developments in the Far East were building up to a situation that was soon to threaten the Massagetae and all other tribes of the Kazakhstan and Central Asiatic steppes. China, under the Chou dynasty, went through a serious crisis which undermined the authority of the central government, and Chinese records show that by the end of the third century BC Central Asia was the scene of sweeping changes, that mark the end of the Early Sarmatian period.

THE PROKHOROVKA CULTURE

In the region of the river Ilek, south of the town of Orenburg, archaeological remains dating from the end of the fifth century BC have been found, which are entirely alien to the local Samara-Ural branch of the Sauromatian culture. They bear a striking resemblance partly to those of central Kazakhstan, but mainly to those of the region on the Syr-Daria delta in the preceding period (see Chapter II), the chief similarities being the construction of the grave-shafts with a niche, or a 'catacomb', for the corpse, and the orientation of the corpse with its head to the

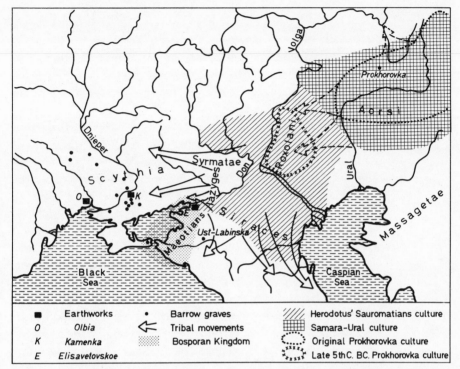

Fig. 28 Distribution of cultures at the end of the fifth century BC. The advance of the newly formed Prokhorovka culture is shown, and the consequent retreat into Scythia and the north Caucasus of the Sauromatian tribes, subsequently known as the Royal Sarmatians (or the Scytho-Sarmatians) and the Siraces (after Smirnov)

south instead of to the west or east. Another new feature in this region derived from the south-east is the so-called 'diagonal' grave, a wide square shaft in which the corpse was laid diagonally.

The appearance of an alien group of archaeological remains in Sauromatian territory is evidently due to the arrival of a new people. The characteristic features of the newcomers' culture point to their having come from the Syr-Daria delta, and suggest that they were one of the Massagetan tribes. This is corroborated by the 'Pamiro-Fergana' racial type prevailing in barrow graves, especially in the Prokhorovka cemetery. The Massagetae were in the ascendant during this period, and subsequent developments in the region of the southern Urals seems to point to some kind of political dependence on the Massagetae on the part of the Sauromatians in that area.

The Massagetae evidently initiated and furthered the transformation during the fourth century BC of Sauromatian culture into a new culture. This, known as the Prokhorovka culture,[2] lost the 'Scythian' quality characteristic of its predecessor and acquired west Siberian (central Kazakhstan) and Central Asiatic features, although many elements of the ancient Sauromatian culture were incorporated in it.

Fig. 28

The Prokhorovka culture was formed in the region of Orsk and Orenburg, within the territory of the eastern division of the Samara-Ural group of the Sauromatian culture, and soon penetrated further west, spreading to the lower Volga area around Saratov. By the end of the fourth century BC almost the entire Sauromatian territory was under its sway, except for the region of Cheliabinsk on the eastern side of the South Urals, where the native population (presumably the Ircae) still kept to the Sauromatian pattern and adopted only a few elements of the Prokhorovka culture. A fresh gain was Bashkiria, the country west of the South Urals, where it reached the town of Ufa.

Two main groups of the Prokhorovka culture have been distinguished, roughly corresponding to those of the Sauromatian culture: the Saratov group on the lower Volga, and, more important, the Orenburg group in the steppe country of the South Urals and the area further south. The formation of these two groups is evidently due to the inclusion of local Sauromatian elements which differed to some extent from each other. The two groups, and also the hybrid Cheliabinsk and Bashkirian groups further north, apparently correspond to different Sarmatian peoples. The Saratov group has been identified with the Roxolani,[3] and the Orenburg group with the Aorsi.

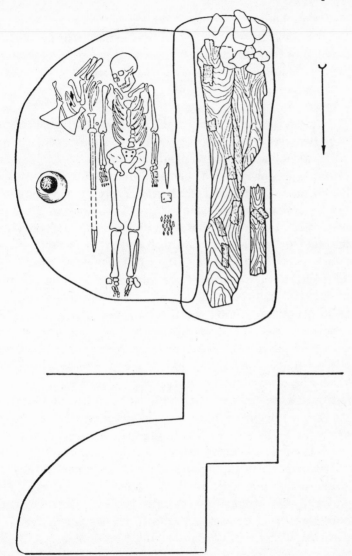

Fig. 29 'Catacomb' grave of the Prokhorovka culture from the region of the River Buzuluk, Orenburg group (after Smirnov)

The Prokhorovka culture is thought to have been common to all Sarmatian tribes of the Early Sarmatian period, which lasted until about the middle of the second century BC. However, several Sauromatian tribes that were forced by the eastern (Massagetan) invaders to abandon their country still retained their ancient culture.

About 550 graves dating from the Early Sarmatian period have been excavated, over 370 of them in the Saratov group, where the mounds contain a large number of secondary burials, evidently serving as burial grounds for a family or clan. The graves are not uniform. Deep, narrow shafts are most common, but wider shafts are also found. Many have a niche in one of the wider sides, but, in the Saratov group larger burial chambers in the southern, narrow end of the shaft (called 'catacombs') are the norm. A small number of 'diagonal' graves were also found. They were always among the best equipped, which suggests that those buried in them, apparently of Central Asiatic stock, held a leading position among the Roxolani and Aorsi, and other subdued Sarmatian tribes. Many graves, especially in the Orenburg group, were covered with small cairns or flat stones; traces of timber constructions have also been recorded, and traces of large hearths around the grave, or over it, are common. Crema-tion burials, mainly on the ancient surface, are characteristic of the Cheliabinsk group, while rather the exception in other groups belonging to the culture. An unusual feature is that every type of grave described appears in all groups of this culture.

Fig. 29

The corpses lay supine with their heads almost exclusively facing south, thus differing from Sauromatian practice. The graves usually contained a single skeleton, although some multiple burials, of a man and woman, or a woman together with one or more children, were also found. Lumps of realgar, chalk, charcoal, or sulphur were often thrown into the shaft, and the bottom was strewn with white clay, sand or ashes from the fires lit around the grave.

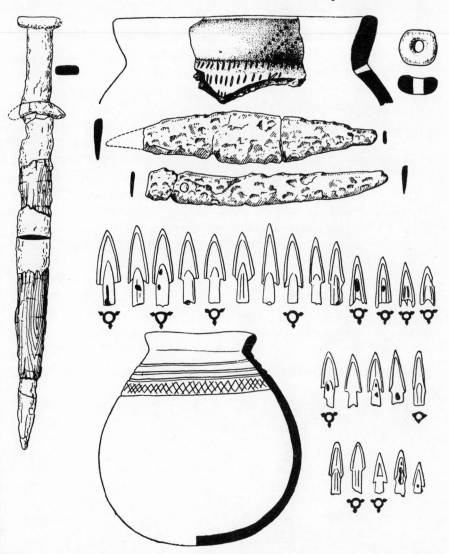

Fig. 30   Objects from a Prokhorovka barrow grave of the fourth century BC at Novyi Kumak near Orsk, Orenburg group (after Moshkova)

Plates 11–13

Pottery—the most common grave good—included ovoid or spherical vases with a short or a high neck and rounded, occasionally flat, base; the beakers had similar features. The decoration consisted of vertical incisions, rows of hatched triangles, concen-

Fig. 30

tric semicircles and like geometric patterns. Many vessels were undecorated.

Male burials were usually equipped with weapons, although arrow-heads were occasionally found in female burials. Arrow-heads were of the 'Scythian' type, socketed and triple-edged, mostly made of bronze, though bone and, at a later stage, flat tanged iron arrow-heads were also common. Swords (mostly

Plates 14–16

long) and daggers formed a substantial part of the armament in burials of Sarmatians of both higher and lower rank. Most had a narrow, crescent-shaped pommel and a straight guard, but the ring-shaped pommel, current during the subsequent period, was already being produced. Occasionally scale armour, or fragments of it, and iron lance-heads, weapons characteristic of armoured cavalry, were excavated. Simple round or oval belt buckles,

Fig. 31

mainly of iron, were among the most common objects found.

Fig. 31 Decorated buckles of the third and second centuries BC of the Prokhorovka culture (after Moshkova)

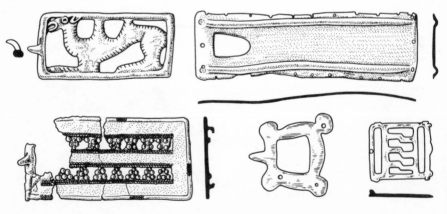

The beheaded carcass of a sheep or a horse, or at least a sizeable portion of it, was usually placed in the better-furnished graves. The most richly endowed burials were uncovered at the barrow grave cemetery of Prokhorovka, thought to be the burial-ground of the leading Sarmatian tribe of that time, or of a royal group.

Female graves contained mainly ornaments and pottery, simple bronze ear-rings and beads being the most common objects. More than 11,000 examples of beads were excavated in the Prokhorovka cemetery, mostly of coloured glass, though semi-precious stones were also used and occasionally bronze and amber. Bronze mirrors, which have usually been ritually broken, were a developed form of those current in the country during the Sauromatian period. Bronze and gold neck-rings and bracelets appeared only in the richer graves.

Fig. 32

Fig. 33

No stone 'altars' typical of the Sauromatian culture were found, but a few decorated stone dishes with a raised rim may be regarded as a survival of this tradition.

The extent to which the grave goods varied, especially in the Orenburg group, points to social differentiation, and the diversity in burial rites and grave-construction reflects the different geographical groups which contributed to the formation of the culture. Furthermore, since these differences occur even within a single cemetery, the heterogeneous composition of the Sarmatian tribes of the Prokhorovka culture is clear.

The close relations between Central Asia and the eastern branch of the Sauromatian culture were considerably strengthened during the Early Sarmatian period. Many of the objects found in various regions of the Prokhorovka territory, chiefly in the Orenburg area, such as wheel-turned pottery and beads made of a variety of stones, were imported from Central Asia or, through Central Asiatic middlemen, from the countries further south. The position with regard to the Saratov group was different. The upheaval at the end of the fourth century BC, caused mainly by the expansion of the Prokhorovka culture, disrupted the ancient

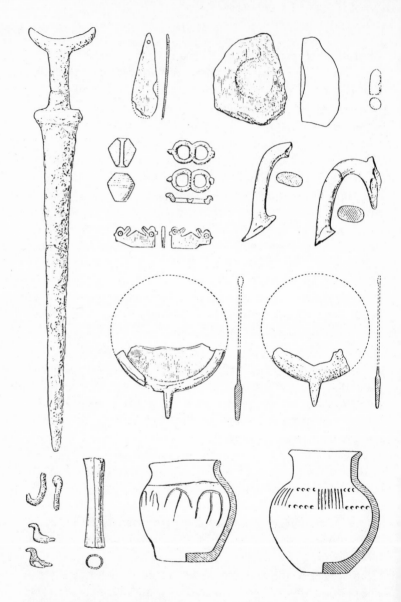

Fig. 32 Objects from barrow graves of the Prokhorovka culture at Kalinovka, Saratov group (after Shilov)

Fig. 33 Bronze and gold personal ornaments of the Prokhorovka culture, third-second centuries BC (after Moshkova)

relations of that area with the northern Caucasus and the Scythian west. Contacts were renewed during the third century, after which black-polished vessels of north-west Caucasian origin, Bosporan red-coloured pottery, and a variety of other goods of the same provenance are found in graves of the Saratov group. A few Greek vases, amulets and glass beads of Egyptian or Phoenician

Plate 17

origin must have been imported through Bosporan intermediaries.

THE BOSPORAN KINGDOM

During the fourth century BC, as the Prokhorovka people
gradually took over the lower Volga region, the local Sauromatians either surrendered or moved west or south. Those who entered
the Pontic steppe and penetrated the area east of the Sea of Azov
as far as the Caucasus, were the first Sarmatians to make direct
contact with the classical world, in the shape of the Bosporan
Kingdom. Some attention must therefore be given to this
kingdom, before we trace the movements of the expelled Sarmatian tribes and piece together their history.

The Bosporan Kingdom goes back to the sixth century BC,
when Greeks, mainly from Miletus, founded several colonies on
the northern coast of the Black Sea and traded with the Scythians
and Maeotians who lived on the eastern shores of the Sea of Azov.
During the sixth and fifth centuries Olbia, situated near the mouth
of the Southern Bug, was the main trading centre. Pottery,
mirrors, gold ornaments, textiles, wine and olive oil, were
among the luxury goods imported from the Ionian cities and the
Greek mainland, or produced in Olbian workshops, and
delivered to the Scythian ruling class.

The Greek colonies extended over both sides of the Strait of
Kerch (the Cimmerian Bosporus of the ancients) and along the
Black Sea coast. Little is known about their earliest period, but
as early as *c*. 480 BC most of the thirty-odd towns and cities had
united for their common protection against the steppe nomads
into a single political organization, the Bosporan state, with
Panticapaeum, modern Kerch, as its capital. However the
Scythians, and after them the Sarmatians, were content to use the
Greek cities as commercial centres.

In about 438 BC, Spartocus, probably a Thracian mercenary
leader, assumed command of the state. His successors, the Sparto-

cids, gradually expanded their territory and at the turn of the fifth century subjugated the Sindians and other Maeotian tribes, and assumed the royal title. Finally, the Bosporan Kingdom embraced all Greek colonies on the shores of the Sea of Azov and a wide stretch of land along the eastern coast, inhabited first by Maeotians, and later by Sarmatian or Sarmatized tribes. A large army of mercenaries, chiefly Greeks and Thracians, was employed, later adding Scythian and Sarmatian cavalry units.

The Bosporan economy was based on trade.[4] Commercial relations were maintained with the Ionian cities and Greece, and in the fifth and fourth centuries corn from the large farming estates in the Kerch peninsula west of Panticapaeum was the chief export to Athens. Exports of fish were also important during the whole period of the Kingdom's existence. By the sixth century many bronze and iron foundries and workshops had sprung up in Panticapaeum and other cities, working for both the home and neighbouring markets. Their products were distributed chiefly among the north Caucasian tribes, and those of the lower Volga steppe, but some reached the Urals and even countries further to the east. In the fourth century BC, Panticapaean exporters won almost all the Scythian territory in the Ukraine which had previously been dominated by Olbian commerce; the change was evidently due to political events to which we shall return later.

Plate 18

The reign of Peirisades I (344/3–310/09 BC) was the most prosperous period of the Bosporan Kingdom under the Spartocids. A war with the Crimean Scythians in 330 BC caused some set-backs, but it was not until somewhat later that a series of events took place which spelt the end of Bosporan prosperity. The conquests of Alexander the Great opened up Western Asia to the Greeks; corn from East Mediterranean countries and Egypt competed with Bosporan products. Furthermore, in 309 BC a civil war broke out in the Bosporan Kingdom after the death of Peirisades I, with a struggle for succession between his sons.

The Sarmatian tribes, newly arrived in the borderland of the kingdom, joined in this war on the side of one of the sons, Emelus, who ultimately succeeded to the throne.

The social and racial development of the Bosporan Kingdom are apparent from the burial practices and grave goods discovered in ancient Panticapaeum and other cities. During the sixth and fifth centuries, the tombs and burial ritual are almost entirely Greek. Graves of the fourth and third centuries BC vary greatly in construction and equipment, and reflect the great prosperity of the Bosporan state at that period, as well as the mixed character of the population and its considerable social differences.

A study of the contents of the graves shows that the Greek elements in the kingdom adhered to Greek ritual and customs. But during the fourth and third centuries a gradual adoption of features characteristic of the surrounding non-Greek population can be discerned, especially in the sumptuously furnished barrow graves of the local aristocracy, most of which were ransacked in antiquity. Several of these (Kul-Oba, Bolshaya Bliznitsa, etc.) are famous for their fine golden objects, which are among the best examples of the so-called Scythian art of the fourth century BC. The role of the Panticapaean master-goldsmiths in the develop-ment of Graeco-Scythian art will be discussed later.

Plates 19, 20

TANAIS

The north-eastern corner of the Sea of Azov was well known to Greek traders at an early date. There, in the Don delta, lies the large earthwork of Elisavetovskoe,[5] covering an area of 40 hectares (about 99 acres), and containing a citadel in which the local aristocracy and Greek merchants lived. The settlement was situated on the island called 'Alopecia' in antiquity. Attached to it was a large cemetery, a few graves of which date from the fifth century BC, the majority being of the fourth, and first half of the third century BC. All the earlier graves have a 'Scythian' character, but the bisected or beheaded carcasses of sheep found in those of the later period imply the presence of a strong Sauromatian element. The settlement thrived on trade with the Sarmatians on the lower Volga and the Scythians on the Don. It ceased to exist by the middle of the third century BC.

In the second half of the third century BC, a new trading city, named Tanais, was founded in the vicinity by the Bosporans. Strabo says that it was an emporium common to the Asiatic and European nomads (Sarmatians and Scythians) and partly Bosporan; slaves, hides and 'such other things as nomads possess' were exchanged there for clothing, wine and 'other things that belong to the civilized life'. The city was divided into two distinct sections, inhabited by the Greeks and the Tanaite-Maeotian natives, but the two communities had a considerable influence on one another. During the first centuries of the Christian era, the whole population gradually became Sar-matian. Tanais had two cemeteries: a barrow-grave cemetery containing the richly furnished graves of the upper class (at first mainly Greek), and the other consisting of the 'flat' graves of the indigenous Tanaites.[6]

THE SIRACES

The presence of the Siraces, a Sarmatian tribe, in the steppe extending south of the Don to the Caucasus, east of the coastal strip inhabited by the Maeotian tribes, is reported in the second half of the fourth century BC. Soon afterwards they took part in the war of succession of 309 BC between the three brothers fighting for the Bosporan throne. Their original country lay on the steppes of the Manych basin, south-east of the lower Don, which they abandoned as they retreated before the Prokhorovians.

Siracian archaeological remains in the early period consist both of princely barrow graves and of 'flat' cemeteries in which the common people, including both rank-and-file Sarmatians and the assimilated indigenous Maeotians, were buried. One of the largest of the second type, at Ust-Labinska,[7] consists of about 250

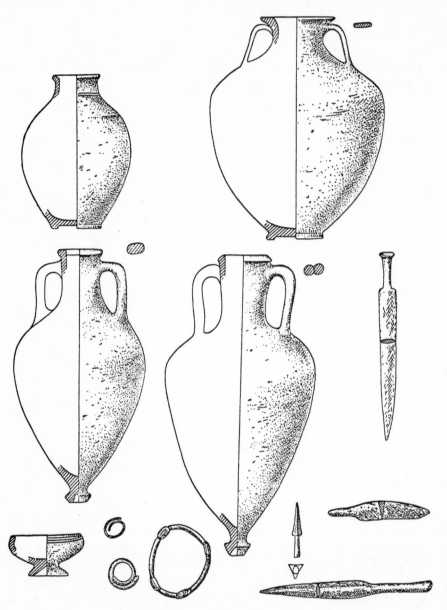

Fig. 34 Pottery, weapons and personal ornaments from Siracian graves of the fourth-third centuries BC in the cemetery at Ust-Labinskaya (after Anfimov)

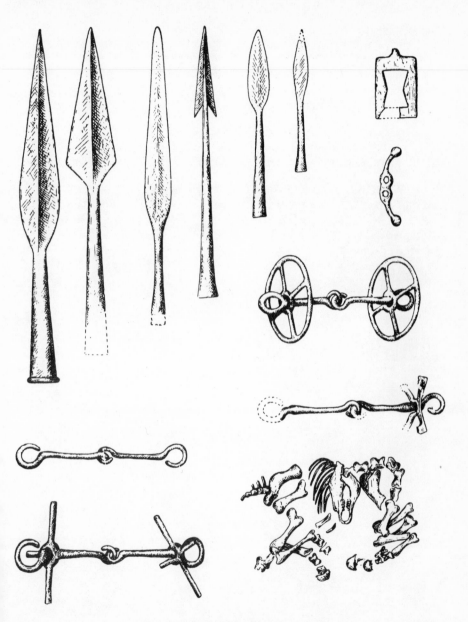

Fig. 35   Lance-heads, horse harness and a horse skeleton from Siracian graves at Ust-Labinskaya, north-west Caucasus. Fourth-third centuries BC (after Anfimov)

graves, the earliest of a 'Scythian' character dating from the sixth to fourth centuries BC, although most are of the third and second centuries, the Early Sarmatian period. The Early Sarmatian graves are mainly of the 'catacomb' type. Wheel-turned pottery forms the main category of grave goods, up to five vessels being

Fig. 36 Examples of the Sauromatian zoomorphic style, north-west Caucasus (after Smirnov)

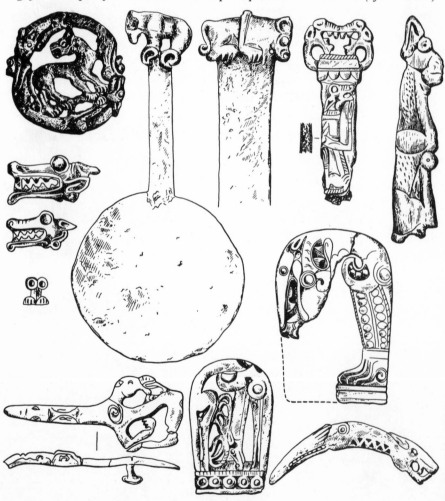

found in a single grave. Wine amphorae of Rhodian and *Fig. 34*
Sinopian origin, bronze bracelets, ear-rings, necklaces of glass,
paste, carnelian, and opal, and from time to time amber beads,
were found in the better furnished graves. Small round mirrors
and flat rounded sandstone plates reminiscent of Sauromatian
altars evidently bore some religious meaning, as did terra-cotta
plates with a Medusa-head and lumps of realgar. Once a Panticapaean coin of the third century BC was found. In male burials, *Fig. 35*
iron knives and whetstones are common, weapons infrequent;
the latter were chiefly iron spear-heads and arrow-heads, but not a
single sword was excavated. Horses were buried near their
masters in a few graves. Bones of sheep, pig and, occasionally,
cattle were among the remains of provisions for the journey to the
beyond.

The nature of the graves in the Kuban area, their furniture and
objects decorated in the Sauromatian animal style, probably *Fig. 36*
brought by them from the north, imply that the Siraces who
settled in the north-west Caucasian steppe were originally people
of Sauromatian culture who had adopted many features of the
Prokhorovka culture, probably from newcomers to their ranks.

Early Sarmatian archaeological remains of the Prokhorovka
type have also been found in Dagestan, in the north-east Caucasus.
Here a heterogeneous local group developed in which intrusive
Sarmatian elements were combined with the culture of the native
Udini, a people mentioned by Strabo.

CHANGING EVENTS IN ANCIENT SCYTHIA

A few rather vague observations are the only extant literary
records relating to the history of the Scythians in the post-
Herodotus period, the fifth and fourth centuries BC, when
considerable changes took place. The Sauromatians from the
lower Volga withdrew not only southwards, but to an even
greater extent westwards. The presence of Sarmatians west of the
Don, in territory which was formerly Scythian, was noted in

338 BC by Pseudo-Scylax, who calls them the 'Syrmatai'. Their arrival may have been earlier, as Pseudo-Hippocrates suggests; according to him the Sarmatians (Sauromatae) had already crossed the Don and entered Scythia by the end of the fifth or the beginning of the fourth century BC. A characteristic Sauromatian grave was found on the lower Dnieper (Hrushivka).[8]

The advance of the Sauromatians in Scythian territory had far-reaching consequences. Evidently under Sauromatian influence the Early Scythian culture of the sixth–fifth centuries BC was replaced by the Late Scythian culture of the fourth to the early-second century BC. The considerable differences between the two stages of the Scythian culture have been emphasized by many scholars. The later stage shows several eastern features previously unknown,[9] for instance burials in deep 'catacombs', or a camel skeleton discovered in a princely burial at Nowosiólka, and graves of women armed in the Sauromatian manner found in the lower Dnieper steppe. Furthermore, study of the cranial material from the royal barrow graves of the Late Scythian period at Alexandropol reveals that the 'royal' skulls are of a type characteristic of the Lower Volga Sauromatians of the preceding period, whereas those of the serfs are typical of the North Pontic Scythians. One skull from the royal burial of Chertomlyk, of the same period, is of a Siberian racial type.

These changes were not the outcome of a peaceful evolution. The Scythian settlements in the lower Dnieper valley destroyed by the very end of the fifth or early in the fourth century BC give archaeological evidence of a troubled period. This suggests that the 'Royal Scythians' described by Herodotus were deprived of their leading position in Scythia at the beginning of the fourth century BC. B. N. Grakov considers that the ancient dynasty was replaced by usurpers, probably princelings of a Scythian tribe on the Don. However, it seems more likely that the Royal Scythians, or perhaps only their rulers, were ousted by the advancing Sarmatians (Sauromatians), while the majority of the Scythians remained, being subdued by the incoming 'Sauromatians' of the lower Volga group, and gradually merging with them. This is suggested by the archaeological material of the Late Scythian period which appears to be a blend of the two elements.

The rulers of the Royal Scythians presumably withdrew westwards with some of their loyal tribes, possibly retaining a narrow belt of steppe west of the Southern Bug for a short period. But their main refuge was Dobruja (that part of Romania between the Danube and the Black Sea) where they appear early in the fourth century BC, their presence being attested by a number of typical Scythian objects dating from the fourth century, which also exhibit many features characteristic of the earlier period. Archaeological evidence seems to support the view that Atheas, mentioned in historical records, far from being 'King of All the Scythians', was only the chief of a branch of the Scythians which had retreated to Dobruja. The Royal Scythians may even have reached Thrace still further south; in any case they exerted a powerful influence on the culture of the rulers in that country.[10]

This upheaval on the steppe adversely affected the commerce and well-being of Olbia. At the turn of the fifth century BC, the city was cut off from its best customers, the Scythians of the Cherkassy group on the middle Dnieper, and its profitable trade with the Urals and the countries beyond ceased altogether. The markets which the Olbians had developed were taken over by the Bosporan Panticapaens, with whom the new eastern rulers of Scythia had had commercial relations in their original country on the lower Volga and Don. Outlets for Olbian trade were now restricted to a narrow strip along the Black Sea coast between the estuary of the Dnieper and the lower Dniester.

THE ROYAL SARMATIANS

The newcomers to Scythia were undoubtedly of 'Sauromatian' stock, probably the original tribe whose name 'Sarmatians' was later applied to other kindred peoples who subsequently moved to the Ukrainian steppe land. The Iazyges, who are first recorded under various names (Iaxamatae, Ixibatai, etc.), and placed south of the lower Don, seem to have belonged to the same group. By the end of the second century BC, Strabo places them in the steppe west of the Dnieper and east of the Dniester. Before migrating there, during the fourth and third centuries, they may have occupied the steppe between the Sea of Azov and the lower Dnieper, where they are placed by Ptolemy. Together with the Siraces, the Iazyges seem to have been the most south-westernly tribes of Herodotus' Sauromatians. Some of the writers of antiquity believed they were Maeotians, but when in the Ukraine they were always regarded as a Sarmatian people: the designation 'Sarmatians' was only occasionally applied to kindred peoples of Iranian stock who later appeared in the North Pontic area— the Aorsi, Alani, and others—and even exceptionally to the Roxolani.

The Ukrainian archaeological material of the period indicates that the incoming Sarmatians (those of Sauromatian culture) mingled with the indigenous Scythians, most of whom remained in the country. They may, therefore, be called 'Scytho-Sarmatians' and it is reasonable to attribute the archaeological remains of the Late Scythian period in the Ukrainian steppe country to them. Some of the early writers call them the 'Royal Sarmatians' and they may also be identified with the 'Basileans' (i.e. 'royal people') whom Strabo mentions as living west of the Dnieper in the second century BC. The title 'royal' was evidently given to those Sarmatians who took over leadership of the tribes of ancient Scythia from the Royal Scythians of the Early Scythian period (the sixth and fifth centuries BC).

During the fourth and third centuries BC—the 'Late Scythian period' in the west and the 'Early Sarmatian period' in the east— the 'Scytho-Sarmatians' took an active part in the few recorded contemporary events. In 331 (or 326) BC, they helped Olbia to ward off Zopyrion, one of Alexander the Great's generals and governor of Thrace, whose siege of Olbia was the most perilous event in her history. The Olbians took energetic steps to mobilize their own forces, but it was the 'Scythians' who rescued the city by defeating Zopyrion's 30,000-strong army. Zopyrion himself fell in battle. Nevertheless, the gradual decay of Olbia set in, and it was accelerated by new tribal movements and changes in the early second century BC.

In 330 BC, we learn, war broke out between the Scytho-Sarmatians and Peirisades I, King of Bosporus, over some territory in the Crimea, probably a strip of steppe-land west of Panticapaeum which had been seized by the Bosporans. But apparently relations between the belligerents later improved. After the death of Peirisades I in 309 BC, a Scytho-Sarmatian army of 20,000 foot warriors and 10,000 cavalry gave its support to one of his sons, Satyrus II, in his struggle for the succession against his brother Eumelus who, backed by the Sarmatian Siraces, was eventually victorious. A few Late Scythian royal tombs were built in the vicinity of Panticapaeum, which seems to confirm that relations were reasonably friendly. They are all of the third century BC, and include the splendid Kul-Oba barrow dating from *c.* 300 BC.

STEPPE BURIALS OF THE FOURTH AND THIRD CENTURIES BC

Neither 'Sauromatian' nor Iazygian remains have so far been positively identified in the Ukraine, but they must be sought among burials attributed to the Late Scythian culture. The tribes which crossed the Don in the fourth century cannot have belonged to the Prokhorovka culture, which is widely regarded as the representative culture of all early Sarmatians, since, when the 'Sauromatian' Sarmatians entered the Ukraine, the Prokhorovka culture was still in its formative stage. The 'Sauromatian' Sarmatians did not differ basically from the Scythians whose country they had usurped and with whom they had obviously merged. Hence their remains are barely distinguishable from those of the indigenous Scythians.

We may therefore attribute to a blend of the Sarmatian (Sauromatian) newcomers with the local Scythians, and possibly also to the Iazyges, burials of the Late Scythian period in the steppe barrow-grave cemeteries. The eastern character of Late Scythian burials on the lower Dnieper has been stressed by several scholars who connect this phenomenon with the influx of Sarmatian and north Caucasian elements; the same applies to contemporary burials on the Molochna and to several barrow graves to the south of Kiev east and west of the middle Dnieper.[11] Their construction and grave goods show several eastern (Ural and Siberian) elements previously unknown in Scythia, as do some aspects of the burial rites. These features all appear at the turn of the fifth century BC, the time of the Sarmatians' entry into Scythia, according to the ancient records. Late Scythian barrow grave cemeteries are found in the areas controlled by the Royal Sarmatians and Iazyges during the period of their occupation, and the latest burials in these, dating from the early second century BC, correspond with the period of Early Sarmatian retreat westwards before the advancing Roxolani (a people of the Prokhorovka culture). These remains are described below.

The graves on the lower Dnieper and Molochna of the late Scythian period—the fourth to early second century BC—are barrow graves: either primary, or secondary in Bronze Age mounds. No interruption in the use of the cemeteries is apparent, which suggests, despite the total absence of burials typical of the sixth and fifth centuries (the Early Scythian period), that the area was continuously settled. This implies, in turn, that the rank- and-file Scythians of the Early Scythian period kept to their ancient Srubnaya culture (of the Late Bronze Age), and that the contemporaneous 'Scythian' culture represented only their rulers and the upper classes. The graves of the Late Scythian period are generally uniform, consisting of rectangular shafts usually provided with a niche, or 'catacomb', placed—unlike those of the Prokhorovka culture—on the wider side of the shaft. Skeletons lay supine, normally with their heads to the west, following the Srubnaya and Sauromatian custom, and only exceptionally to the north. Of cremations there is no indication. Male burials were equipped with weapons, including wood or leather quivers with up to 100 bronze arrow-heads, sometimes iron lance-heads and, rarely, a dagger or short sword. A few contained a silver ear-ring. Sherds of hand-made local ware, cups, vases, handled dippers, etc., were also found. There were a few bone objects and small metal plates adorned in the Scythian animal style. Bones of horses, cattle or sheep were common, usually left in a heap with an iron knife sticking out of the top. There were no horse sacrifices but in a few cases bronze cheek-pieces and bits were discovered.

The female burials were no less modestly furnished, with animal bones and potsherds, together with pieces of broken saddle-querns and personal ornaments such as bronze, or very occasionally silver, ear-rings, bracelets, occasionally a pin, and exceptionally a mirror with a handle. The most common objects are necklaces of beads which are usually made of glass or paste, occasionally of amber or bone, and only exceptionally of gold. In a few female graves arrow-heads were found, but they were rarely in a quiver. Two burials in particular are remarkable. A female burial in the catacomb of a barrow grave at Kut, west of the lower Dnieper, yielded an iron sword and a quiver with thirty-six arrows; other goods included a bronze mirror, bronze ear-rings and ornaments and a necklace of glass beads. The other, at Akermen on the Molochna, was a catacomb-burial of a young woman, equipped with a bronze mirror, a necklace of glass beads, silver, bronze and glass bracelets, a few wooden vessels and a Greek amphora. Beside her were two iron spear-heads and two lance-heads, a quiver with twenty arrows, and a suit of scale armour. She is thought to have been the Sarmatian wife of a Scythian. A few female burials of the sixth, and also of the fourth century BC, equipped with arrow-heads have been found in the forest-steppe zone of the Ukraine.

Fig. 37

A number of well-known, sumptuously furnished 'royal' burials of the Late Scythian period have been discovered in the same area. They correspond in their basic plan to the graves of the common people, but are far more lavishly equipped. Not only have they far more elaborate and better finished niches and 'catacombs', but they incorporate human and horse sacrifices never found in the graves of commoners.

The equipment of the Late Scythian royal tombs differs markedly from that of the royal tombs of the Early Scythian period. No objects of Transcaucasian, Oriental or Olbian origin are found in them. All the fine gold and silver vases, gold-plated dagger grips, scabbard covers and quivers, etc., are now Bosporan, Panticapaean products, or else imported from Thracia or from Mediterranean countries via the Bosporan ports. New, however, are the large cast-bronze cauldrons of a Siberian type. A princely female burial at Nowosiólka, east of Vinnitsa, contained the skeleton of a camel, evidently brought from the steppes of Kazakhstan.

This striking change in the type and equipment of royal burials points to important changes in Scythian society, especially in the ruling class. Two graves are of primary significance: first, the famous barrow grave of Chertomlyk situated near Nikopol north of the lower Dnieper. This has been described in many publications, but it has seldom been mentioned that its equipment included three cast-bronze cauldrons of the Siberian type, and above all, that an anthropological examination has revealed that the king was of Siberian extraction.

Less well known is a similar royal burial of the mid-fourth century BC discovered recently in the town of Melitopol,[12] in the centre of the area presumed to have been occupied by the

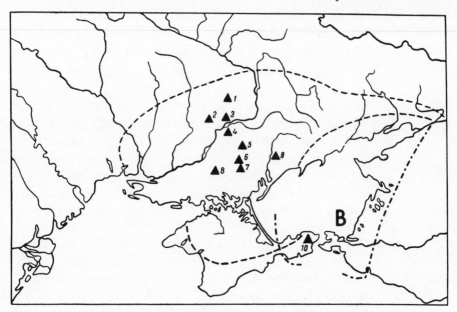

Fig. 37   The Ukraine during the Late Scythian (Early Sarmatian) period, fourth-third centuries BC. 1 Alexandropol; 2 Raskopanaya Mogila; 3 Chertomlyk; 4 Solokha; 5 Chmyrev; 6 Ogüz; 7 Deev; 8 Mordvinovskii; 9 Melitopol; 10 Kul-Oba; B the territory of the Bosporan kingdom around the sea of Azov; triangles represent richly furnished 'Late Scythian' (Scytho-Sarmatian) princely or royal barrow graves; the broken line shows the territory within which the 'Late Scythian' catacomb or niche graves appear (after L. S. Klein)

Iazyges during that period. This might have been the tomb of an Iazygian ruler. It had two 'catacombs'; in the central one—which was ransacked—lay the king with his attendants and two horses, in the other a woman. The king's equipment consisted of an iron pick-axe, iron scale-armour, bronze arrow-heads and many small gold plates originally sewn on to a garment. A hiding-place, undiscovered by the looters, contained a bow-case   Plate 21
with a covering of gold decorated with scenes from the life of Achilles—a replica of gold plaques found in barrow graves of

Chertomlyk, Illintsy near Vinnitsa and the barrow grave of the Elisavetovskoe in the Don delta, all dating from the second half of the fourth century BC. Remains of saddles, iron cheek-pieces and bits, and bronze ornaments from the horses' harness were found near their skeletons. The female grave had been partly

Plate 22

looted, but Greek red-varnished vases, gold, glass and paste beads, bracelets and finger-rings were found, together with remains of a funeral cart and its yoke, a bronze cauldron and eleven amphorae. It should be pointed out that very few objects decorated in the genuine Scythian animal style were found in either of the two graves mentioned above or in other tombs of this group; most of the fine silver and gold vases, plaques and orna-ments were Bosporan products, their decoration only slightly adapted to the taste of the nomad princes.

Both royal and common burials of the Late Scythian period in ancient Scythia are of a mixed character. Besides local features, their tomb construction, ritual and equipment, show a marked Sauromatian element as well as specifically Siberian features. Burials of the south Ural type with Siberian elements dating from the turn of the fifth century BC have also been found in the Ukrainian forest-steppe zone on both sides of the Dnieper. As an example may be mentioned a fourth-century BC grave of a Sarmatian commoner of the 'Sauromatian' group, excavated at Ushkalka on the lower Dnieper, about 30 km. west of the Kamyanka earthwork.[13] The complex character of the graves reflects the heterogeneous composition of the population of the Ukrainian steppe at this time, consisting of indigenous Scythians and some 'Sauromatian' tribes from the lower Volga steppe, among them possibly the Syrmatai and the Iazyges. Eastern features exhibited by the royal tombs suggest that the leading positions in the Scytho-Sarmatian ruling class were held by a group of Central Asiatic, or Kazakhstan, extraction, who were presumably among the initiators of the Prokhorovka culture in the southern Urals.

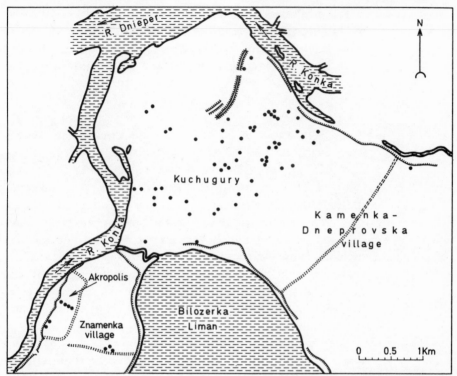

Fig. 38   Plan of the 'Scythian' earthwork at Kamyanka-Dniprovska (Znamenka-Znamyanka) (after Grakov)

THE KAMYANKA EARTHWORK

Several fourth-century BC settlements have been discovered in the lower Dnieper valley, from the region of the rapids down to Kherson.[14] All were abandoned by the beginning of the second century BC. Only two have defensive constructions: the Belozerka earthwork near the mouth of the Dnieper, and the Kamyanka earthwork on the southern bank of the Dnieper opposite Nikopol, an area of 1200 hectares (3000 acres) enclosed by the Dnieper, the Konka and a lake called Liman Belozerskii. Its two relatively narrow entrances were barred by huge ramparts and dykes.

Fig. 38

109

This earthwork consists of two parts, the smaller of which, over 32 hectares (about 80 acres) in area and irregular in plan, is situated on the narrow causeway between the lake and a branch of the Konka; it has been called the Znamenka earthwork, or the 'Acropolis', and was surrounded by a strong supplementary rampart strengthened on top by hard-baked bricks.

Each section of the earthwork fulfilled a different purpose. The larger was a major industrial and metallurgical centre, which, as recently established, relied on the supply of local bog iron ore. The complex of workshops, foundries and forges included living-quarters. The nature of the waste material indicates that what was made there was intended not only for the steppe nomads and the agricultural tribes that occupied the near-by river valleys, but also for their upper classes. The products included tools, weapons, simple ornaments, etc., of types often excavated in the barrow graves of the surrounding region. A few objects decorated in the Scythian animal style indicate that at least some of the items found in the steppe graves were of Kamyanka manufacture.

The 'Acropolis' on the other hand shows no traces of metallurgical activity, which suggests that it was the administrative centre and seat of the rulers of the Late Scythian people. The many imported objects, especially wine amphorae, found in both sections of the earthwork show that relations were maintained with the Bosporan cities. The industrial centre appears to have operated only during the fourth and third centuries BC; there is no sign of any activity in the second century. The 'Acropolis' was inhabited for rather longer, but ultimately became merely one of the series of earthworks along the lower Dnieper.

That the Kamyanka earthwork was the administrative centre of the Scytho-Sarmatian kings in the Late Scythian period seems to be corroborated by the rather unusual concentration of lavishly furnished barrow graves on its perimeter on both sides of the Dnieper, described in the preceding section.

SCYTHO-SARMATIAN TWILIGHT

After lasting for almost two centuries the era of Scytho-Sarmatian prosperity came to an end. No richly furnished royal barrow graves have been discovered in the vicinity of the Kamyanka earthwork later than the second half of the third century. The Scythians (or Scytho-Sarmatians) were forced to abandon the earthwork at the beginning of the second century BC. Pressure from kindred Sarmatian peoples east of the Don, particularly the Roxolani, compelled the Scytho-Sarmatian rulers to leave the country east of the Dnieper; some of their subjects retreated west of the river, but their main refuge was the Crimea. There, the kingdom now known as the Tauro-Scythian or Crimean Scythian Kingdom came into being, a blend of Scythian, Sarmatian and Taurian ethnic elements with an admixture of Greek. In addition to ruling the Crimea itself, the Crimean kings retained control over a narrow strip of steppe surrounding the estuaries of the Dnieper and the Southern Bug around Olbia.

The Roxolani now became the leading power in the North Pontic area. Their appearance in the steppe east of the Dnieper marks the beginning of a new era, the Middle Sarmatian period.

CHAPTER IV

The Middle Sarmatian Period

Second century BC to mid-first century AD

TURMOIL IN THE ASIATIC STEPPES

AFTER TWO CENTURIES of more or less peaceful development in the Early Sarmatian period, new tribal wars and
displacements at about the turn of the third century BC, reported
by both Greek and Roman writers and in Chinese chronicles,
mark the beginning of the new era.

Late in the third century BC, the Chinese had to build the
Great Wall of China, which in 214 BC was partly finished, to
protect their country against the inroads of the Hunnic tribes.
In 209 BC, a strong Hunnic tribal union was formed under Mode
(209–174 BC). We learn that in 201 BC Mode conquered the
country of Dinlin, located in the Minusinsk valley on the
Yenissey; the Dinlin have been identified with people of the
Tagarskaya culture. This account is corroborated by archaeological evidence which shows that by the end of the third century
the Tagarskaya culture had been replaced by a new and entirely
different culture, the Tashtyk, represented, it is thought, by one
of the Turcoman peoples who lived under Hunnic overlordship.
Fateful events then took place on the eastern border of the
Kazakhstan steppes. The Yüeh-Chih and Wu-sun (Usuny),
most probably Tocharian speaking peoples,[1] were defeated by
the Huns and their countries overrun. Sections of both these
peoples ceded their lands to the victors and, in retreating westwards, set in motion the Sacian tribes.

Fig. 39   The archaeological material from Semirechie, the regions on
the Upper Irtysh and the Upper Ob, formerly the easternmost
Iranian—Sacian and proto-Sarmatian—countries, indicates considerable changes in the composition of their populations by the

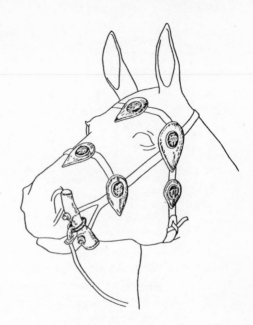

Fig. 39   Bridle from barrow grave 12 at Biisk on the upper Ob. Reconstruction (after Zavitukhina)

Fig. 40

end of the third century BC.[2] Certain similarities between the intrusive cultures in these areas and that of the Altai Mountains (Pazyryk) and the country of Tuva in the preceding period suggest that the newcomers, who fled under Hunnic pressure, may have come from those regions.

The large tribal union of the Massagetae was also affected by the Hunnic advance. At some time between 174 and 160 BC, or in 165 according to some authors, they were defeated by the Huns and forced to abandon their country. The evidence of both the ancient authors and the archaeological remains point to a massive migration of Sacian-Massagetan tribes from the Syr-Daria delta by the middle of the second century BC. Some of the Syr-Darian tribes were among the Iranians who, by conquering Bactria in 135 BC, ended the Graeco-Bactrian Kingdom; they also invaded North India.

The Huns' striking successes in overcoming neighbouring peoples, including the Sacians and the Massagetae, were probably

113

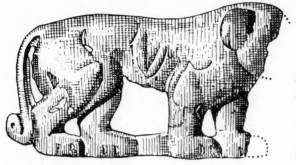

Fig. 40   Massive bronze plaque in the shape of a tiger or panther, from a barrow grave of the first century BC/AD in the cemetery at Berezovka near Biisk on the upper Ob (after Poltoratskaya)

Fig. 4

due to the use of the new, extremely efficient 'Hunnic type' of bow.[3] It was larger than the Scythian type hitherto widespread among the steppe peoples and was made of several pieces of different kinds of wood strengthened by bone inlays. The arrows were longer, with triple-edged, tanged heads of iron. These weapons gradually rendered armoured cavalry obsolete in the Asiatic steppe country.

The Hunnic victories, and in particular the downfall of the Massagetae, started the wholesale abandonment of the Kazakh-stan and Central Asiatic steppes by the Iranian-speaking nomads, a process that took more than five centuries, continuing until about the fourth century AD.

THE AORSI

Early in the second century BC, when the easternmost part of the Kazakhstan steppes was subdued by the Huns, the 'Early Nomads' of central Kazakhstan formed the vanguard of the Sarmatian tribes facing the enemy.

The archaeological remains in central Kazakhstan and adjoining areas indicate considerable changes at the beginning of the second century BC,[4] when a new period corresponding to the Middle Sarmatian in the Urals and on the Volga began. The mounds become smaller and lower, and contain a niche or dromos in which the corpse was buried with its head to the north-west. The grave goods consist of small vessels, up to 12 cm. high,

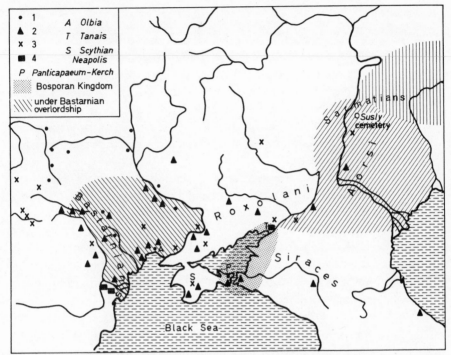

Fig. 41 Eastern Europe during the Middle Sarmatian period (second century BC–mid-first century AD). The Early and Middle La Tène finds show the extent of Celtic (Bastarnian) influence; the area of assumed Bastarnian overlordship over western Ukraine and Bessarabia in the second century BC is shown. 1 Early La Tène brooches; 2 Middle Tène brooches and other small objects; 3 La Tène swords and helmets, and Celtic graves in Romania and Carpatho-Ruthenia; 4 Celtic oppida in the Danubian delta

iron knives, bone awls, a variety of pendants, beads of paste and stone, and occasionally of gold. Exceptionally, there are stone dishes or bowls.

These changes were brought about by a new wave of Iranian-speaking newcomers retreating westwards before the Hunnic menace. As in the past, some tribesmen remained in their country, mingled with the newcomers, and were gradually absorbed.

Fig. 41

Others yielded to the pressure and moved west with the result that the region of the southern Urals and the lower Volga steppe were similarly affected. The newcomers to these areas, the territory of the Prokhorovka culture, initiated what is known as the Middle Sarmatian period. It probably began early in the second century BC and lasted until about the middle of the first century AD, although some authors date the arrival of the eastern invaders *c.* 135–130 BC.

It seems that the invaders came mainly from central Kazakhstan, but the culture of those who settled in the steppe-land south of the Urals, as far as the Caspian Sea, shows close parallels with that of contemporary peoples in Semirechie, a country east of Lake Balkhash bordering on Chinese Turkestan. We may assume, therefore, that the newcomers included tribes from that area, who must have travelled about 1900 km. (some 1200 miles) to reach the steppe north of the Caspian Sea.

The dominant group of the Middle Sarmatian period in the lower Volga and southern Urals area was known to the ancients by the name of 'Aorsi'. They may have inherited this name from the preceding period, since some scholars maintain that it was applied to the originators of the Prokhorovka culture in that region.[5] The newcomers subdued the local Sarmatians and put an end to their Prokhorovka culture.

The eastern origin of the Aorsi, and their consanguinity with their eastern neighbours, the Alani of central Kazakhstan, are suggested by their name, which in Iranian means 'the Whites': in the language of all ancient steppe-dwellers 'white' means 'western'. The 'Western Alani' was the name applied to them by their kindred, and even by some ancient authors. They were an Iranian people of purely Andronovo ancestry, unlike the Syrmatae, the 'Royal' Sarmatians, the Iazyges, and probably the Roxolani, who were descended from the Late Bronze Age Srubnaya people with a fairly comprehensive admixture of Andronovian blood. Nevertheless, they must have absorbed a substantial part of the people of the Prokhorovka culture. The centre of power of the Aorsi lay around Orenburg and Orsk, within the eastern division of the northern group of the Middle Sarmatian culture. Their rise began with the decline of the Massagetae around 160 BC, and they subsequently subdued all the Sarmatian tribes of the Volga-southern Urals region, or forced them to migrate westwards into the North Pontic steppes. Among the migrants were undoubtedly the Roxolani who at that time appeared on the lower Dnieper, compelling the 'Scytho-Sarmatians' and Iazyges to retreat west (see Chapter III).

The Aorsi are mentioned in the Chinese *Annals of the Former Han* (about 138–126 BC) under the name of 'Yen'ts'ai' or 'An'ts'ai' (Antae), possibly the name of their leading tribe. With a force of 100,000 archers, they were regarded by the Chinese as a mighty people dwelling somewhere between the Aral Sea and the Caspian. In 125 BC, a Chinese legation tried to incite them against the Huns in order to relieve pressure on the Chinese borders, which seems to imply that the territory held by the Aorsi, or by peoples subordinated to them, bordered on that ruled by the Huns.

Strabo, in the early first century AD, mentions a people called the 'Upper Aorsi' in the southern Urals and describes an important trade route running through their territory by which Indian and 'Babylonian' merchandise was imported on camels and exported to the Medes and Armenians south of the Caucasus. This trade was a source of wealth for the Aorsi, who 'could afford to wear gold ornaments'. However, the relationship between the 'Upper Aorsi' and their branch on the lower Volga and Don, called by Strabo 'the fugitives of the Upper Aorsi', remains obscure.

Judging by the equipment of princely barrow graves on the lower Volga near Volgograd (e.g. Kalinovka) and the lower Don, and the large hoard of golden personal ornaments found further south (Kozinskoe, *c.* 100 km. south-east of Stavropol),

Plates 23–26

the Aorsi seem to have been a powerful people with wealthy rulers. Spaldines, their king, raised an army of 200,000 horsemen which took part in the Bosporan Kingdom's dynastic struggle in 64–63 BC, and we hear of a Sarmatian legation, evidently Aorsian, 'from a country on the Don', arriving in Rome during the reign of Augustus (23 BC to AD 14). In AD 49 Eunones, King of the Aorsi in the Don⁄Volga region, was an ally of the Romans and of Cotys, the newly enthroned Bosporan ruler.

THE MIDDLE SARMATIAN CULTURE

With the upheavals of the beginning of the second century BC begins the Middle Sarmatian period, characterized by the Middle Sarmatian, or Suslov, culture.[6] It was a period of cultural assimilation, but the division into two main groups is neverthe⁄less still marked, although the two branches, called the Orenburg group in the north, and the Volga⁄Ural River group in the south, do not correspond exactly to the two main branches of the pre⁄ceding Prokhorovka culture in the Early Sarmatian period. The Orenburg group extended over the steppe country east of the Volga near Saratov as far as the region of Orenburg and Orsk; the territory of the southern group (of the Aorsi) was the steppe between the lower Volga near Volgograd and Astrakhan and the lower Ural River. Smaller regional groups can also be dis⁄tinguished within the two main groups. In the northern group there is a marked difference between its western division on the Volga, and the eastern division around Orenburg and Orsk. In the southern branch of the culture the Suslov group of cemeteries (named after the barrow⁄grave cemetery at Susly on the Volga) exhibits special features of its own. A number of settlements and flat cemeteries on the lower Don may also be included in this branch.

Typical of the southern branch are low mounds containing up to 100 secondary burials—evidently forming the burial⁄ground of large family groups or clans. All the varieties of grave dis⁄

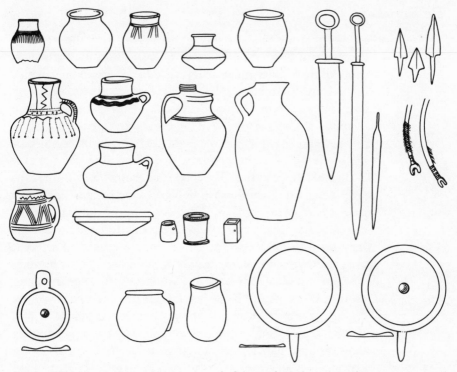

Fig. 42   Pottery, weapons and mirrors typical of the Suslov culture (Middle Sarmatian period) from the lower Volga (after Abramova)

tinguished in the Early Sarmatian period in the same area are found, but most common is a shaft with a niche or 'catacomb'. 'Diagonal' graves are also frequent, amounting to 30 per cent of the total number of graves in the Suslov cemetery, which seems to have been the burial-ground of a ruling tribe. The skeletons lay supine, with their heads pointing south, and occasionally in some regions, west; a few deformed skulls were found. The corpse was usually sprinkled with lime or chalk. Cremation, total or partial, was exceptional.

The survival on the lower Volga of burial rites characteristic of the eastern group of the preceding Prokhorovka culture implies that the tribes of this group moved from the region of the southern Urals into the lower Volga region. Furthermore, a study of the cranial material reveals that the group was mainly of the 'Europoid brachycephalic' type which most anthropologists connect with the Central Asiatic 'Pamiro-Fergana' type common among the people of the Prokhorovka culture.

Fig. 42

Grave goods from all the Sarmatian territories show only minor variations. Long swords with a spherical pommel of glass or chalcedony were gradually replaced by short swords and daggers with a ring on top of the grip in place of the pommel. Spear- or lance-heads are exceptional. But it is only by the end of the period that the Sarmatians east of the Volga had abandoned heavy armed cavalry and fought either on horseback or on foot, principally armed with the new bow introduced by the Huns.

Fig. 43

Many grave goods reflect Central Asiatic connections: mirrors, bone spoons, horse harness, red-coloured pottery of the Kushan type and distinctive jugs with an animal-shaped handle. Jewellery, including gold plates set with coloured stones or glass, show striking parallels to objects from Siberian burials in the Hermitage Collection; the latter have usually been wrongly

Plates 27–30

dated to the earlier periods. Graves on the lower Volga, especially those of the Suslov group, indicate relations with the Bosporan Kingdom; here the objects include jewellery, brooches of various types made sometimes of silver, including the tendrilled type 'with the foot turned over' deriving from those introduced by the Celts (the Bastarnae), glass, carnelian and amber beads, Egyptian-type faience pendants and amulets, Roman terra-sigillata vases, wheel-made pottery of Kuban or Bosporan provenance, etc. Small bronze (sometimes gold) plaques sewn on to garments are common to the whole Sarmatian region. Gold, apart from the plaques, is rare. Fragments of sheep bones are often found in a dish or bowl, but entire carcasses are now the exception.

There is a relatively large group of archaeological remains from the Middle Sarmatian period in the area from the lower Don

Fig. 43 Jugs with zoomorphic handles and bowls from Siracian graves at Ust-Labinskaya, north-west Caucasus. First century BC to second century AD (after Anfimov)

south to Manych and eastwards; they probably extend as far as the Volga delta. The remains consist of several fortified settle-ments along the Don, barrow graves and 'flat' cemeteries. Most of the inhabitants of the settlements were probably descendants of tribesmen who lived in the region during the preceding periods, but some were Sarmatians who gradually adopted a settled life. All were farmers, but stock-rearing played an important role in their economy, and some of the settlements had close connections with the city of Tanais.

THE BOSPORAN KINGDOM

The conquest of the eastern division of the North Pontic steppes by the Roxolani early in the second century BC weakened the Bosporan Kingdom's economic and political situation. The large Pontic market was lost, and at the same time the Sarmatian and Scythian menace grew. The Bosporans were forced to pay tribute to the Crimean Scythians, who by the middle of the second century had increased their demands. The Bosporan King, Peirisades the Last, being unable either to pay or to resist the 'barbarians', sought the protection of Mithridates VI Eupator, King of Pontus, a country on the south-eastern coast of the Black Sea.

In 110 BC Mithridates' armed force under Diophantes defeated the aggressors, and Scythian Neapolis was seized. Events then moved quickly. In 107 BC, Peirisades was killed during a rising of the Scythian and Sarmatian inhabitants of Panticapaeum; so ended a dynasty which had survived almost four hundred years. Mithridates seized the Bosporan Kingdom for himself, thus involving it in his wars with Rome. After his death in 63 BC, a peace lasting nearly fifteen years ensued but subsequently a new phase of dynastic feuds opened. They were concluded by the middle of the first century AD, with the establishment of a new dynasty of mixed Sarmato-Thracian origin, members of which bore mainly Thracian or Sarmatian names, 'Sauromates' being one of them. This dynasty ruled until the onslaught of the Goths in the fourth century AD.

Plate 32

The peace treaty with the Romans, concluded by Pharnaces, Mithridates VI Eupator's son and successor, and his daughter Dynamis, conceded suzerainty over the Bosporan Kingdom to the Roman Empire. This was chiefly nominal, although from time to time a Roman garrison was stationed in Bosporan territory. The kingdom was regarded as an important outpost of the Empire against the steppe nomads and was therefore supported and protected.

THE SIRACES IN THE KUBAN REGION

The Siraces in the Kuban valley and the steppe north of the north-west Caucasus (see Chapter III) seem to have been the only Sarmatian peoples not to have moved out of their country by the end of the Early Sarmatian period. They were not numerous; Strabo says that in about 66–63 BC their King Abeacus had at his disposal only 20,000 horsemen, whereas Spaldines, King of the Aorsi, who were their northern neighbours, had 200,000.

The territory of the Siraces adjoined that of the Bosporan Kingdom, and their rulers were often involved in its internal affairs. During the dynastic feuds of AD 49, Zosines, King of the Siraces, supported Mithridates VIII, a great-grandson of Mithridates VI Eupator against his half-brother Cotys in alliance with Rome. Several battles were fought, in which the Aorsi also took part as allies of the Romans. Ultimately both Mithridates and the Siraces were defeated. Zosines, in order to save his ancestral kingdom, sought peace and became a tributary of Rome.

No further written records concerning the Siraces are extant, but the survival of the kingdom until the end of the second century AD is attested by an inscription at Tanais announcing a victory of the Bosporans over the Siraces in AD 193. The years from AD 49 to AD 193 were probably relatively peaceful, a period during which close relations with the Bosporan Kingdom resulted in the Siraces becoming the most Hellenized of the Sarmatians, while at the same time contributing largely to the Sarmatization of the Bosporan Kingdom. In fact the equipment of Siracian upper-class graves is barely distinguishable from that of the Bosporan aristocracy.

The Siraces were partly pastoral semi-nomads, wagon- and tent-dwellers, and partly settled farmers. Many of their permanent settlements, usually hill-forts, have been found in the Kuban valley, where their houses were made of beaten clay. The inhabitants practised both arable farming—wheat, barley and

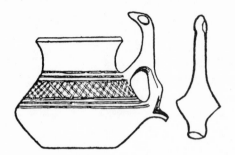

Fig. 44 *Sarmatian clay vessel with zoo-morphic handle (a bird) from Kerch-Panti-capaeum (after Skalon)*

millet were grown—and stock-raising. Cattle, horses, sheep and pigs were kept, and fishing was important in their economy. Their settlements were also centres for handicrafts which were strongly influenced by the Bosporans. It was a rigidly stratified society. At the top were the kings and the princes, heading a hierarchy of social classes, with widely differing grades of wealth and privilege.

Our knowledge of Siracian life derives chiefly from a study of their graves which, again, are of two types—the 'flat' cemeteries where the mass of the people were buried, and the princely barrow graves, confined to the upper classes.[7]

The largest of the flat cemeteries is at Ust-Labinska, which the Siraces used from the time of their arrival in the country in the fourth century BC. Graves of the Middle Sarmatian period are less numerous, and there are differences between the type and equipment of these burials and those of the earlier period, due to the influx of newcomers from the north (the lower Volga) at the beginning of the period.

The pottery is mainly wheel-turned ware—bowls, globular vessels, etc.—but the most characteristic objects are jugs with handles in the form of animals, or with the top of the handle shaped like an animal's head. Jugs of this type are common among the Sarmatians on the lower Volga and the steppes further east, and in the Bosporan kingdom; they were probably adopted from Central Asiatic peoples, who produced jugs with zoomorphic handles from the second century BC on.

Fig. 43
Fig. 44

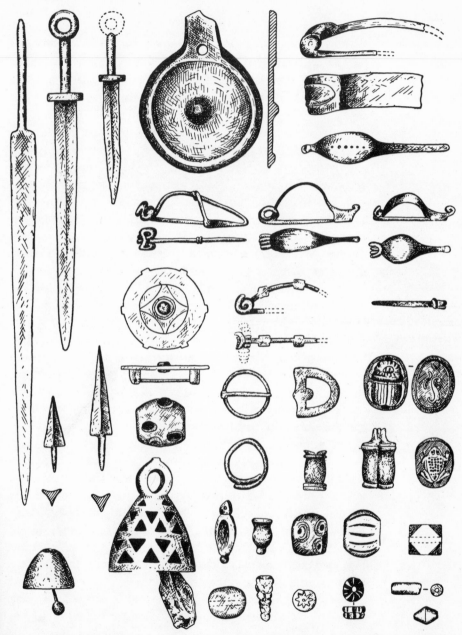

Fig. 45   Weapons, ornaments, Egyptian scarabs, a late Sarmatian mirror and other objects from graves in the Siracian cemetery at Ust-Labinskaya. First century BC to second century AD (after Anfimov)

Fig. 45
Weapons are more numerous than before. The daggers and swords are of two types—either long and narrow, or short, double-edged and pointed. Iron spear- or lance-heads are common, but the socketed arrow-heads are replaced by three-edged tanged points. Jewellery is also plentiful, including the characteristic 'Sarmatian' tendril fibulae 'with the foot turned over', and brooches of the 'arlabest' type which were typical mainly of the Late Sarmatian period. The mirrors are usually decorated. Richly furnished graves contain imported goods—glass vessels, terra-sigillata bowls, beads made of glass, paste and semi-precious stones, and Egyptian scarabs and figurines. In most graves animal bones, usually of sheep, occasionally of cattle or pigs, were found. Sometimes there were complete skeletons, usually of cows, seldom of horses.

Plate 31
The variations in equipment of the 'flat' graves reflect the social position and wealth of the people buried in them. But there is far more difference in this respect between the flat graves and the barrow graves. The Kuban barrow graves, which are far richer than the graves of other Sarmatian groups of the period, were evidently burials of the Siracian upper class. They include such well known examples as the barrow graves at Ust-Labinska near the flat cemetery, those at Vozdvizhenskaya and Armavir, and the Zubovskii barrow grave.

The princely barrow graves are usually small with a grave-shaft above a niche. Sometimes a man only is buried, sometimes a man and woman are buried together. The construction and funeral ritual recall Sarmatian graves on the Ural steppe where the newcomers probably originated. The equipment has a local, Kuban and oriental character. Some of the grave goods do not differ from those of the flat cemeteries, but gold objects and imported goods are plentiful. Another difference is that all those buried in princely graves were horsemen.

The principal weapons are heavy, long lances and long swords with a wooden grip, oval in section, topped by a round or

square pommel of some precious or semi-precious stone. Both
men and horses wore corselets, but by the end of the first century
AD scale corselets are replaced by ring-armour. Conical helmets
were found in several graves. Wall paintings of Bosporan knights   *Fig. 5*
in the 'catacomb' tombs depict them well armed in just this
manner, and so does the well known Triphons stele from   Plate 33
Tanais. Bows and arrows played a secondary role in the armament
of these knights. The trappings of their horses differ from those of
the Scythian period, but phalerae were still in use. The bits have
simple rings, and stirrups are found for the first time in these
tombs.

Jewels and ornaments have been found in quantity—torques,
fibulae of the same types as those in the flat graves, diadems and
bracelets. Belt-buckles and clasps are mostly of openwork, often
with coloured filling. With polychromy (related to Persian and
Georgian goldsmiths' work), the animal style became considerably modified by the filling in of the animals' bodies with gems
and cut pieces of coloured glass, and enclosing them in a coloured
frame. Small thin metal (usually gold) plates sewn on cloth are
very characteristic, hundreds of them having been excavated from
Kuban barrow graves. They differ from those of the Scythian
period in being very small and geometric in shape—discs,
triangles, crescents, rosettes, etc., all of an oriental type.

Some of these objects were products of Bosporan (mainly   Plate 34
Panticapaean) workshops, but others were of local Siracian
manufacture. Others again came from even farther afield—
Greek goods imported through the Bosporan town of Panticapaeum, and oriental luxuries (especially beads) which reached
the country by the caravan routes described by Strabo. As well
as jewellery, Iranian and Indian ideas must have followed the
same route, considerably influencing Siracian culture and that of
other Sarmatian tribes.

Two objects recovered from Kuban barrow graves are of Greek
origin and can be dated to the sixth century BC, i.e. five centuries

or so before the graves in which they were found. According to an inscription on one of them, they originally belonged to the Temple of Apollo at Phasis and were evidently looted in the course of a raid south of the Caucasus.

THE WEST: THE BASTARNAE

Some attention must be paid to the Bastarnae, a Celtic people, called at first the Galatians by ancient writers, who—around 280 BC—crossed the Carpathians and settled in the country on the Dniester and the Pruth, reaching the delta of the Danube. In about 240–230 BC, Trogus Pompeius mentions that the Bastarnae live on the middle Dniester and near the Danubian delta. During the second century BC they became the dominant people of the area. Mingling with the indigenous Getae, the Scythians and Sarmatians, with whom they intermarried freely, they soon became a people of mixed blood.

Fig. 40

Attributable to the Bastarnae are a number of genuine La Tène finds from the area that—according to the ancients—was held by them.[8] Early and middle La Tène objects found in settlements and earthworks along the middle Dniester near Rybnitsa and Rezina presumably mark the eastern border of the Bastarnae in the third century BC. At the turn of the Middle Sarmatian period, the Bastarnae seem to have penetrated further eastwards, up to the Dnieper, as suggested by Celtic La Tène brooches and other objects found west of the river. Noteworthy is a princely burial with several Celtic La Tène objects of the period around 100 BC found at Marievka-Bougalom on the Southern Bug, and also a 'Scythian' barrow grave near Tarashcha, south of Kiev, in which a La Tène iron sword of *c.* 200 BC was excavated. La Tène swords of the same period have also been found in princely tombs in Scythian Neapolis in the Crimea.

Fig. 46

Dacian pottery of the so-called Carpatho-Danubian type, peculiar to settlements of Bessarabia and Moldavia, the territories at that time held by the Bastarnae, was found in the settlements and

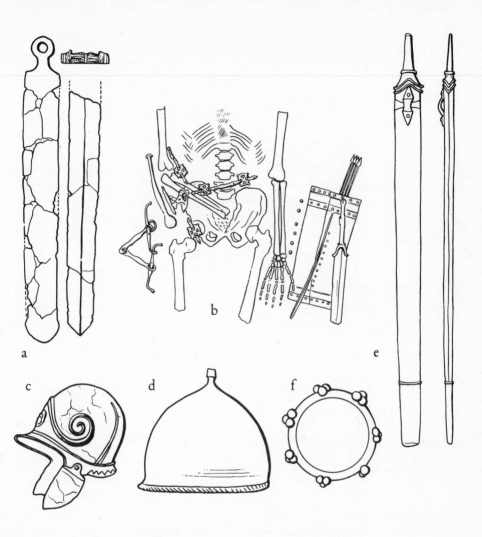

Fig. 46 Celtic weapons found in eastern Europe: a, Middle La Tène sword from a burial in the 'Mausoleum' at Scythian Neapolis; b, iron sword, horse harness and a quiver in situ *from the same burial; c, helmet from the same burial; d, La Tène bronze helmet from Bugakom-Marievka near Nikolaev on the Southern Bug; e, Middle La Tène sword from a grave at Verkhne-Tarasovka on the middle Dnieper; f, bronze ring of the fourth-third centuries BC from a princely barrow grave at Prusy near Smela in the Ukraine (after Pogrebova)*

earthworks of the second century BC along the Dnieper.[9] It suggests that the Ukraine west of the Dnieper was then either under some sort of Bastarnian control, or that the rulers of the nomad Scythians in the steppe, like those of the presumably Thracian-Getan tribes in the black-earth area further north, were allied to the Bastarnae. It seems very likely that the collapse of the Scytho-Sarmatian rule in the North Pontic area by the end of the third century BC made the Bastarnian penetration easier, and that the presence of the Bastarnae on the Dnieper prevented the in-coming Roxolani to cross the Dnieper and seize the country west of the river.

The culture of the peoples of the Ukraine and the Crimea[10] (or at least that of their rulers) was influenced by the La Tène culture represented by the Bastarnae. Well defined traces of similar influence are noticeable also in the culture of the Sarmatian tribes in the steppe east of the Dnieper as far as the Volga. Its vestiges are Celtic swords, helmets, but above all the wide adoption of Celtic brooches which underwent there a further development that led to the evolution of the so-called brooches 'with the foot turned over', a specimen very characteristic of the Middle Sarmatian culture and period.

THE WEST: THE CRIMEAN KINGDOM

The arrival of the Early Sarmatians in the Ukraine in the fourth century BC does not seem to have had much bearing on conditions in the Crimea. The most important trading centre of the western, 'Scythian' part of the peninsula was Chersonesus, a Greek city founded by the Heracleans by the end of the fifth century BC, with ten to fifteen thousand inhabitants. The city lay on the western coast of the Crimea, close to modern Sevastopol, near the border between the Scythian steppe-nomads and the Taurians of the mountains to the south.

In the second century BC, the seizure by the Roxolani of the steppe-land between the Don and the Dnieper forced the Scytho-

Sarmatian rulers to abandon the Kamyanka earthwork on the lower Dnieper (see Chapter III). The royal seat was transferred to the Crimea where King Skilurus founded the city of Scythian Neapolis on the site of an existing Scythian fort on the southern border of the steppe, in the Taurian foothills near modern Simferopol.[11]

Scythian Neapolis, strongly fortified, became the commercial, cultural and political centre of Scythia. Greek influence was strong; a number of public buildings had colonnades, the remains of which have been excavated, along with many fragments of marble statues and reliefs portraying Kings Skilurus and Palakus. Several inscriptions, exclusively in Greek, were found on the reliefs. The cemeteries lay outside the city; one consisted of caves in which mural paintings of the Bosporan type were discovered. Members of the royal family and the local aristocracy were buried in a 'mausoleum' in the centre of the city. Seventy-two burials were found here, ranging from the late-second century BC to the end of the second century AD. They were in stone or wooden sarcophagi, most of which are richly decorated. In male burials weapons of the Sarmatian type are the main equipment—of special interest is an iron sword of the Middle La Tène type. The female burials are richly furnished with gold ornaments, brooches, bronze mirrors, beads and pendants, Egyptian scarabs, etc. Several Scythian coins of King Skilurus struck in Olbia were found in the ruins of the city, which was eventually destroyed by the advancing Goths in the third century AD.

With the establishment of the Crimean Scythian (in fact Scytho-Sarmatian) Kingdom the position of the Greek colonies within its range deteriorated. The kings, deprived of the vast resources of ancient Scythia, sought revenue by imposing heavy tributes on the Greek cities including Olbia. The decree in honour of Protogenes, an important epigraphical document of *c.* 200 BC found in Olbia, reveals that the Olbians were forced to pay—in gold, which was donated by Protogenes—tribute to a

Fig. 47 Scythian bronze coins minted in Olbia: above, from the reign of King Kanitus; below, of King Skilurus (after Grakov)

Sarmatian tribe, the Sai, and to Saitapharnes, 'King of the Scythians' (evidently the Crimean Scythians). Some of the kings, such as Skilurus in the second century BC, and Farsoi and Inismei in the first and second centuries AD, lived in the city and *Fig. 47* the Olbians had to strike their coins. In spite of this, the Scythians were unable to protect the city in the mid-first century BC, when it was assaulted and destroyed by Burebista, the Dacian king.

The Crimean Scythians seem to have been subordinate to the Roxolani, who at that time ruled over the whole territory between the Dnieper and the Don. The records show that in 179 BC the Chersonesians asked King Pharnaces of Bosporus for help against the Scythians and the Roxolani who occasionally intervened on their behalf. In the middle of the second century BC, the Scythians tried to recover a coastal strip which had been appropriated by the Chersonesians, but their most dangerous venture was an attempt, in 110–109 BC, to seize Chersonesus, when Palakus, the son of the Scythian King Skilurus, captured two small Chersonesian coastal towns, Gavan and Kerkinitida. As we have seen, the Chersonesians sought protection in a treaty with Mithridates VI Eupator, King of Pontus, who accordingly sent an army under Diophantes. The war ended in disaster for the Scythians and their allies the Roxolani, Scythian Neapolis being taken by Diophantes.

After Mithridates' death in 63 BC, all the Greek cities in the Crimea and the Bosporan Kingdom found themselves within the Roman sphere of influence. In the first century AD, a Roman garrison was stationed in Chersonesus, defeating the Scythians who attacked the city. The garrison was temporarily withdrawn, but during the second and third centuries Chersonesus was the Roman Empire's main stronghold in the Crimea. By the end of the third century AD, the Romans had pulled out. The Goths had conquered much of the Ukraine and penetrated the Crimea.

THE WEST: THE IAZYGES

During the Early Sarmatian period the Iazyges lived north-west of the Sea of Azov, between the Dnieper and the Don (see Chapter III). Behind them, east of the Don, on the lower Volga, were the Roxolani. Early in the second century BC the Roxolani, under pressure from the Aorsi, abandoned their country for the North Pontic steppe, forcing the peoples who lived there to retreat across the Dnieper. While most of the 'Scytho-Sarmatians' withdrew to the Crimea, the Iazyges migrated westwards into the lower Dniester steppe.

In their new country the Iazyges had the Bastarnae (La Tène Celts) to the north and north-west, although their closest neighbours were the Tyragetae (the 'Dniester Getae') and other tribes of the Getae in Dobruja. In pushing further south, along the coast, some of the Iazygian tribes must have reached the Danube delta. They allied themselves with Mithridates VI Eupator, King of Pontus, in his war against Rome. We hear that in 78–76 BC there was a Roman punitive expedition against the Iazyges north of the Danube, obviously a reprisal for an Iazygian incursion into Roman territory. This was the first of many recorded encounters between the Sarmatians and Romans. Soon afterwards the Iazyges seem to have been forced to withdraw northwards and any further expansion was checked by the powerful Dacian Kingdom which reached its peak in the first half of the first century BC under Burebista. In about 50 BC Burebista advanced as far as the lower Southern Bug and destroyed Olbia. The city was rebuilt but it covered only about one-third of its former area and its population was halved; it never regained its former position and wealth.

After Burebista's death the Iazyges were again able to reach the Danube, but conditions there had changed. During the first century BC the Romans had established their frontier along the whole length of the lower Danube. The Iazyges often tried to cross it, and invasions, usually undertaken in conjunction with the Dacians, are reported in AD 6 and again in AD 16. Ovid, who from AD 8 to 17 was banished to Tomi (modern Constanta), a Greek city on the western coast of the Black Sea, then in the Roman province of Lower Moesia, has left us several accounts of the Iazyges.

The way south was blocked; but the Bastarnae having been shattered by the Dacians under Burebista, the way west lay open, and soon after AD 20 the Iazyges crossed the Carpathians and settled in the Hungarian Plain and in southern Slovakia.

THE ROXOLANI

On the heels of the Iazyges came the Roxolani. At the outset, in the second century BC, they lived east of the Don, and their movements closely followed those of the Iazyges, whom they pursued across the Dnieper. They are described in about AD 17–23 by Strabo, who calls them 'wagon dwellers' and places their winter camps near the Sea of Azov; in summer they lived in the plain further north. They hunted deer and wild boar in the marshes, and wild asses and roe-deer on the steppes.

The Crimean Scythians were soon forced to acknowledge the suzerainty of the Roxolani, who subsequently became all-powerful in the North Pontic area, although the 'Royal Sarmatians', or 'Scytho-Sarmatians', probably helped by the Bastarnae, succeeded in halting their advance on the Dnieper. The submission of the Crimean Scythians was apparently connected with the activities of Galatus, 'King of the Sarmatians'; he was presumably King of the Roxolani, whose tribal identity was not recognized by the Greeks for some time after their arrival in the North Pontic area. Galatus was allied with Crimean Chersonesus which had probably sought his protection against the Crimean Scythians. His power and prestige are illustrated by the fact that he is mentioned in the peace treaty concluded about 179 BC by the King of Pontus with his adversaries. The subordinate status of the Crimean Scythians is again shown a few decades later. We hear that, between 165 and 140 BC, Amage, a Sarmatian queen, acting for her disabled husband, intervened when her vassals, the Crimean Scythians, attacked Chersonesus. She put the rebellious Scythian king to death, appointed his son in his place and ordered him to live in peace with the Greeks.

About 110 BC, the Roxolani under their King Tasius were again involved in Black Sea politics, allying themselves with the Crimean Scythians against the Bosporans. As we have seen, they were defeated by the Pontic general Diophantes. The Roxolanian detachment is reported to have been 50,000 strong, but Strabo says that though they were reputed to be warlike, they were lightly armed and could not withstand a well-ordered and well-armed phalanx of the Pontic army.

Next we hear that in 107 BC the 'Reuxinali', a Sarmatian tribe presumably identical with the Roxolani, were among the auxiliaries who helped Mithridates in his conquest of the Bosporan Kingdom. The change in Roxolanian policy probably resulted from their defeat by Diophantes, when they were forced to provide the Pontic King with mercenaries.

The rise of the Dacian Kingdom under Burebista in the mid-first century BC marked the end of the Bastarnian predominance in

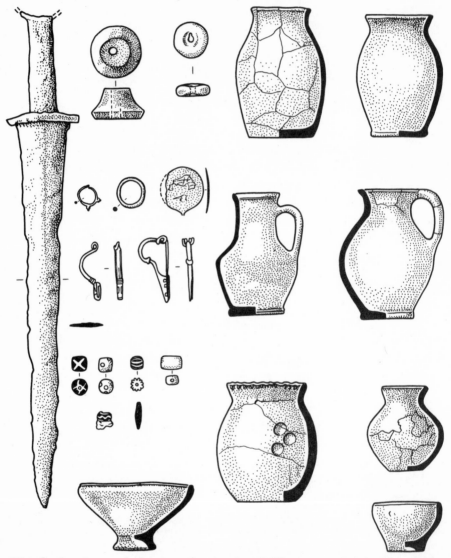

Fig. 48 Sword, personal ornaments and pottery from Middle Sarmatian burials of the early first century AD from Ostrivets near Stanislav in western Podolia (after Smishko)

the country west of the Dnieper. Thus two centuries after their arrival in the North Pontic steppe, the Roxolani were able to cross that river. No description of the migration exists, but it seems to have been caused by the surge across the Don of a new wave of Sarmatian tribes represented by the Aorsi and their kin retreating before the Alans. The movement of the Roxolani shadowed that of the Iazyges whom they again displaced, as they did about two centuries previously. They probably settled somewhere in the steppe between the Dnieper and the Danube delta. A small detachment seems to have proceeded further west, reaching the Carpathians. A Sarmatian cemetery, the most *Fig. 48* north-westerly hitherto discovered, excavated at Ostrivets south of Horodenka,[12] can perhaps be attributed to the Roxolani, or perhaps the Iazyges, who settled there in the first century AD. Its grave goods are typical of Sarmatian burials of the first century AD in the North Pontic area. Another of the Prokhorovka tribes, possibly a branch of the Roxolani, turned north, into the region south of Kiev. Entering fertile agricultural country, they subdued its population and established themselves there for nearly four centuries. It seems plausible to identify them with the Spali, a Sarmatian people mentioned by Pliny, and also by Jordanes.

A large branch of the Roxolani must have turned south and established themselves in the Walachian plain, close to the Roman frontier. Their presence there is reported in AD 62–63 when, in conjunction with the Dacians, they invaded Roman Moesia, only to be hurled back across the Danube by the forces of the governor, Platinus Silvanus.

The advance of the Roxolani deep into Dacian territory displaced the indigenous tribes. Consequently 100,000 Dacians ('Transdanubians') were allowed to settle in Roman Moesia between AD 62 and 66. The Roxolani were far from quiet neighbours, and their incursions into Roman territory are often reported in the years which followed, but they belong to a fresh chapter in Sarmatian history.

ARCHAEOLOGICAL REMAINS

More than two hundred Sarmatian burials of the Middle Sarmatian period have so far been found between the Don and Dniester.[13] They fall into several groups reflecting the existence of distinct tribes whose identification is seldom feasible.

Several graves of the period have been found in the region of the Don and the Donetz. The pottery is similar to that of the Prokhorovka culture, as is the only bronze mirror to be found in a grave on the Donetz. However, the skeletons in these burials lay with their heads to the west, thus departing from the Prokhorovka custom, presumably owing to the absorption by the

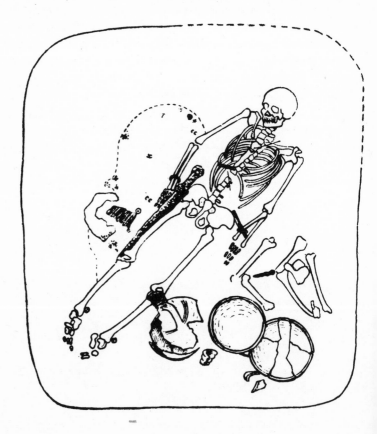

Prokhorovka newcomers of local tribes of Scythian or Sauromatian ancestry.

A number of Middle Sarmatian barrow graves, attributed
to the Roxolani, have been excavated in the steppe north-west of
the Sea of Azov, between the lower Dnieper and the Molochna.
The earliest go back to the late second century BC, but the majority
have been dated to the first century BC and the first century AD.
In their ritual and furniture they are almost identical with those
of the Saratov people of the Prokhorovka culture. We may assume,
therefore, that the people buried in these mounds were driven from
their original country on the lower Volga. They adhered to their
ancient culture, rites and customs for a time, although these had
meanwhile been replaced by customs characteristic of a new period
in their former homeland. Several types of graves occur within
a single cemetery, as in the Volga area during the preceding
period, including the 'diagonal' type, although the majority

Fig. 49

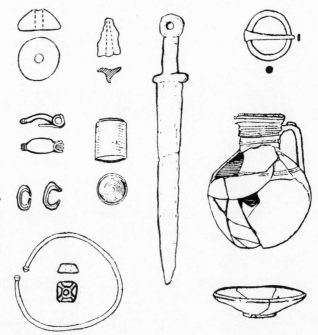

*Fig. 49 A 'diagonal'
grave in barrow 2 at Novo-
Pylypivka near Melitopol,
and its grave goods. First
century AD (after Obol-
dueva)*

consist of narrow shafts with a niche. In most cases the heads point south. The grave goods are again similar, comprising the equipment of lightly-armed mounted archers: iron swords, small iron arrow-heads, quivers made of birch bark, etc. Only the pottery is different, showing many features in common with the local ware found in 'Late Scythian' earthworks on the Dnieper.

Another group of barrow graves of the period has been excavated on the lower Dniester in the region of Tiraspol.[14] The graves are mainly of the 'catacomb' type, and in construction, burial ritual and grave goods correspond to those of the lower Dnieper region in the Late Scythian period. They have been dated to the period from the fourth to the second century BC. The people buried there could indeed be descendants of the Early Scythians, possibly a branch of the 'Royal Scythians' ousted from their original territory on the lower Dnieper at the turn of the fifth century. But it seems more likely that they were a branch of the 'Scytho-Sarmatians' who by the end of the third century BC had to retreat there before the invading Roxolani, retaining their ancient culture and burial rites, only slightly admixed with new elements characteristic of the later period. Hence the group may be considered a conservative branch of the Middle Sarmatian period, a view corroborated by the fact that the majority of its burials date from the second century BC. The group survived until the first century BC as indicated by a number of burials, and may therefore be identified with the Iazyges whom ancient authors place in this area at that time.

Plate 35

Finally, mention must be made of gold and silver-gilt horse trappings and *phalerae*, disc-shaped and covered with embossed geometrical or animal-style decoration reminiscent of ancient Assyrian or Ionian styles, but at the same time closely connected with Graeco-Indian art.[15] They have been found in nine sites, mainly within the southern part of Sarmatian territory west of the Don and in the north-west Caucasian area. One site, however, Tobolsk on the Irtysh, east of the Urals, lay far outside that territory, as did two larger hoards found in areas west of the Sarmatian region; one of these, in south-east Transylvania, contained fourteen *phalerae*, and the other, on the Danube in Bulgaria, yielded six examples.

The *phalerae* found in the north Pontic area were probably produced by Panticapaean silversmiths and goldsmiths. Their decorative style suggests that their introduction in the North Pontic area was in some way connected with the arrival in the Crimea, late in the second century BC, of the Pontic army under Diophantes and with the Mithridatic wars of the first half of the first century BC. The territory within which almost all the North Pontic *phalerae* were found was then in the possession of the Siraces and the Roxolani, both of whom were involved in the war against Diophantes and/or Mithridates' conquest of the Bosporan Kingdom.

Plate 36

CHAPTER V

The Late Sarmatian Period

Mid-first to fourth century AD

THE ALANS

THE PREDOMINANCE OF the Aorsi in the steppes on the borders of Asia and Europe ended by the middle of the first century AD. The Chinese *Annals of the Later Han* (AD 26–211) record that the 'An'ts'ai' (the Aorsi) were re-named 'Al'lan'ai' (the Alans) and this implies that they must have lost their leading position among the Eastern Sarmatians to the Alans. The name 'Aorsi' ceases to be mentioned in western written records, and instead we find some ancient writers referring to 'Alanorsi'. 'Western' or 'White' Alans, possibly denoting the branch of the Aorsi vanquished by the Alans. In AD 68 the Alans were reported in the vicinity of the Sea of Azov, and their arrival was followed by the fortification of the city of Tanais. By the beginning of the second century AD, they were masters of areas previously held by the Aorsi, and of the greater part of Siracian territory. Some of the Aorsi moved west; others accepted Alanic rule and, merging with the newcomers, lost their identity. Some of the Siraces, too, seem to have retreated west, but most of them probably remained in their country, to be subjugated by the Alans and subsequently conquered by the Goths.

The advance of the 'Eastern' Alans west of the Don was probably checked by the Aorsi who had retreated there, and so further attempts at expansion had to be southwards. They sought to conquer Parthia in AD 73–74, probably advancing along the eastern coast of the Caspian, but they failed in this attempt. About AD 123 they invaded Roman territory in north-eastern Asia Minor, but were repelled by the forces of the provincial governor, Arrianus. Another southern incursion is

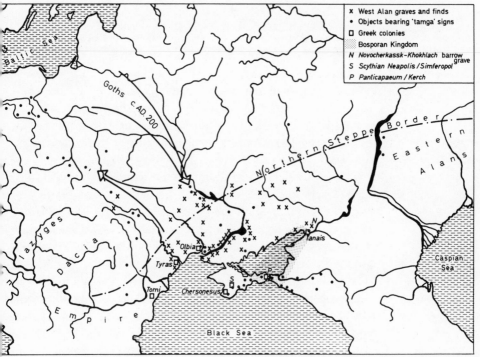

Fig. 50 The Late Sarmatian period (mid-first–fourth century AD) in south-east Europe. The advance of the Goths and the spread of tamga signs into Poland in the third century AD is shown (after Vyazmitina, Solomonik, Nadolski and Sulimirski)

reported in AD 133, and Josephus, the Jewish historian (AD 37–95), has left an account of one of the Alanic border raids in the first century AD, into modern Persian Azerbaijan and Armenia.

The Alans who entered the lower Volga steppe were the rear-guard of the Iranian Sarmatian peoples who gradually abandoned the Asiatic steppes under Hunnic pressure. They were evidently of mixed stock. Ammianus Marcellinus remarks that the Alans (the 'Halani') were once known as Massagetae. 'By repeated victories they gradually wore down the peoples whom they encountered and incorporated them under their own national name.' These tribes, or peoples, 'although widely separated from

Fig. 50

each other and roaming over vast tracts' were 'all called Halani because of the similarity in their customs, their savage mode of life, and their weapons'.

The changes in Eastern Sarmatian leadership and the con-sequent westward migration of several of the Sarmatian tribes were again—as in the past—the outcome of new developments in the Siberian-Kazakhstan steppes, particularly the expansion of the Huns.

The Huns, who according to Ammianus Marcellinus 'ate, drank, slept and held counsel on horseback', were the fieriest and most ruthless of all the nomad peoples who hurled them-selves upon the west. During the first century AD, they seem to have seized the whole of the Asiatic steppe country, including the last Sarmatian-Alan foothold in the south Urals. The Alans, who lived there, mostly retreated to the lower Volga steppe, thus depriving the Aorsi of both country and leadership; although outside Hunnic rule, they were strongly influenced by the Huns and adopted many of their customs.

THE LATE SARMATIAN CULTURE

The extent of the Hunnic impact on the Eastern Alans is reflected in the differences between archaeological remains of the Late Sarmatian culture,[1] and those of the Middle Sarmatian period. The changes had been gradual, and first reached fruition in the eastern part of Alanic territory, north of the Caspian Sea; further south, in the steppe-land west of the Caspian Sea and in the north-east Caucasus many features characteristic of the preceding period, especially burial rites, survived almost to the final stage of the Late Sarmatian period.

Burial ritual now tended to be more uniform over the whole of Alanic territory, the most common type of grave being the narrow shaft usually with a niche or 'catacomb'; 'diagonal' graves almost entirely disappeared east of the Volga. The corpses were laid mostly with their heads pointing north, and the custom

Fig. 51 Sarmatian burial with legs crossed from a barrow grave at Bakhchisaray in the Crimea, second century AD. a, red clay vessel; b, fabric (? felt); c, iron plate with traces of gold inlay (after Kris and Veymarn)

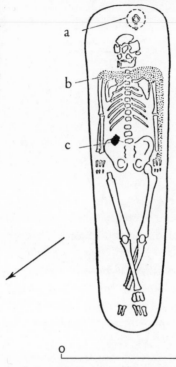

0   1 m

of sprinkling the grave with chalk was discontinued, except in the extreme south. Legs were often crossed now. One Late Sarmatian feature characteristic of the steppe east of the Volga is the deformation of skulls. The custom of binding the child's head to make it grow into a particular shape is found in various prehistoric periods and cultures. It was occasionally practised in the Manych steppe west of the Caspian Sea in the second millennium BC, and deformed skulls are sometimes found there in later burials, including those of the Middle Sarmatian period. The practice became common in Central Asia in the first centuries of the Christian era and was adopted at that time by the Alans and Huns alike. Some 70 to 80 per cent of skulls in Late Sarmatian cemeteries in the Volga and Ural steppes are artificially deformed.

Fig. 51

145

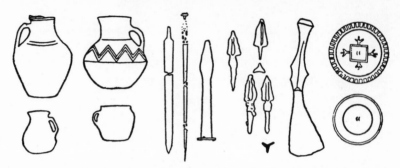

Fig. 52

Fig. 52 *Pottery, weapons and mirrors from Late Sarmatian burials on the lower Volga (after Merpert)*

Fig. 52

The grave goods, particularly the weapons, for the most part represent eastern, Siberian and Central Asiatic types of the period. Long iron swords, long composite bows of the Hunnic type and Hunnic arrows predominate; the horse trappings and bits are likewise Hunnic. The hand-made pottery, especially the cuboid 'incense burners', comprise Central Asiatic types, and the small, round bronze mirrors with a square, perforated handle somewhat differing from those of the preceding period are also of eastern provenance.

The eastern features, hitherto unknown in the area, were brought by a new wave of eastern invaders. They point to close connections between the Eastern Alans and the Huns and other Central Asiatic peoples. According to ancient writers, Hunnic power had by the end of the first century AD extended westwards to the Caspian Sea. Hunnic racial elements (skulls of a Mongoloid character) are found even further west in Sarmatian cemeteries. The possibility that the Eastern Alans of the Volga steppe were politically dependent on the Huns cannot be ruled out.

Fig. 53

However, Bosporan goods, jewellery, Roman enamelled brooches, tendrilled brooches 'with the foot turned over' of La Tène derivation referred to previously, beads of glass and paste, wheel-turned pottery and other similar objects, still appear in graves on the Volga steppe, mainly in richly furnished princely burials.

Fig. 53 Silver strainer, two bronze rings ornamented with camel figurines and a red clay vase, found in a female princely burial of the early second century AD at Bolshaya Dmitrievka near Saratov (after Maksimov)

They imply that despite the overthrow of the Aorsi, the old ties connecting the Volga steppe with the Bosporan Kingdom and the north-west Caucasus were not severed.

The Siraces were also affected. The old cemeteries of the north-west Caucasus which had been in continuous use for more than eight centuries were abandoned; the burial ritual and equipment are now different, suggesting the arrival of new tribes in the second century AD. The culture of the newcomers, the Eastern Alans, who brought about these changes, nevertheless diverged to some extent from that of their kinsfolk who settled on the Volga. It was a blend of Alanic elements with those characterizing the indigenous non-Sarmatian population of the north-west Caucasus. Perhaps the strongest influence, however, was the Siracian culture of the preceding Middle Sarmatian period, reflected in the position of the corpse, the burial rites, and even in certain characteristic grave goods. The newcomers must have assimilated many of the indigenous inhabitants, probably of Maeotian origin, and also the majority of their predecessors, the Siraces. Some forms of pottery and other goods suggest that they maintained contacts with ancient Albania on the other side of the Caucasian Mountains.

Two finds from the lower Dniester area are significant since they imply that some of the Siraces withdrew under Alanic

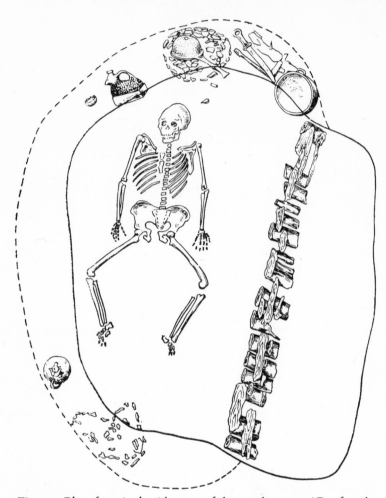

Fig. 54 *Plan of a princely niche grave of the second century AD, of north-west Caucasian (Siracian) type, from Oloneşti near Tighina-Bendery in Bessarabia (after Meliukova)*

pressure and migrated westwards.[2] At Traiany near Balta were found objects typical of the Middle Sarmatian period in the Kuban region. Presumably part of the equipment of a princely burial, they include a bronze mirror and a bronze kettle, or vase, with zoomorphic handles dating from the late second century AD.

Of about the same date is another richly furnished barrow grave, presumably a Siracian royal or princely burial, at Oleneşti near *Fig. 54* Tighina-Bendery in Bessarabia, about 160 km. south of the other. Among its grave goods are three bronze vessels and an enamelled brooch, all of Gallic or Pannonian origin, four wooden vessels with zoomorphic handles typical of the Middle Sarmatian culture in the Kuban region, and a clay zoomorphic vase (shaped like a ram) probably of Olbian origin. The weapons consist of swords, the shorter of them provided with a ring instead of a pommel, an iron spear-head and an iron battle-axe. Parts of richly decorated horse harness were also found.

THE BOSPORAN KINGDOM

The first two centuries AD, and to a lesser extent the third, were a period of great prosperity for the Bosporan Kingdom, thanks to Pax Romana round the Black Sea and the gradual settlement of the Aorsi. There was a renaissance of craftsmanship, which had been at a high level in the fourth and third centuries BC, but had declined considerably during the last two centuries of the pre-Christian era. The work of the Panticapaean goldsmiths became famous once again and, as is indicated by the frequency with which it is found in their graves, it was popular with the local aristocracy and the neighbouring Sarmatian princes.[3] The fine gold and silver jewellery of the later period is distinguished by its predilection for polychromy achieved through the highly skilful use of precious and semi-precious stones and enamel of different colours, glass and paste, combined with filigree braid work, a trend which dates from the end of the third century BC, when it was prevalent throughout the classical East, the Iranian world, Transcaucasia (Georgia),[4] Central Asia and West Siberia. As adapted by Bosporan craftsmen it combined local traditions and technical skill going back to Scythian times with new elements introduced by the Sarmatian newcomers from the steppes of Asia. This style was later adopted and modified further by the Goths, spreading westwards during the migration period, and becoming the basis of the early medieval style in Western Europe.

The culture and internal condition of the Bosporan Kingdom were greatly influenced by its proximity to the Scythians and Sarmatians and by the centuries of peaceful co-existence with them. Sarmatian, or Scythian, elements are visible everywhere in its political and social organization, in its army and in its religious traditions. The ruling dynasty and the majority of the aristocracy were of Thraco-Sarmatian origin. The wealthy middle classes, engaged mainly in trade and industry, were chiefly of Greek origin, but a large part of the population consisted of indigenous Maeotians, Thracians, Scythians and Sarmatians. Despite considerable efforts on the part of the Greek element in the population, the Bosporan state failed to retain its Greek character, although the official language continued to be Greek. The presence of foreign slaves and Sarmatian settlers, attracted by city life, contributed further to this swing away from Greek. Inter-marriage with both Sarmatians and Crimean Scythians acceler-ated the Iranization of the whole population, and the kingdom finally assumed an almost completely Sarmatian character in the first centuries AD. The course of events in the city of Tanais was similar.

This picture is painted by writers of the early Christian era, and supported by the archaeological remains. The family graves of the Bosporan aristocracy in rock-cut chambers bear definite non-Greek features. Sepulchral stelae with sculptures in relief and paintings in grave-chambers indicate a society trying to be Greek but overtly Sarmatian. The Bosporans wore a thoroughly Scytho-Sarmatian dress: trousers, soft leather shoes and long cloaks probably made of wool. Their armour was also Sar-matian: the Bosporan nobles are depicted as cavalrymen with a conical metal helmet, a corselet of scale or ring armour, a long lance, a dagger with a ring on the top fastened to the leg, a sword

with a round stone pommel, a bow and bow-case and a small
shield. The Sarmatian figures on Trajan's Column, or on the
Arch of Galerius at Salonica, are dressed and armed in the same
fashion. The infantry usually wore no corselets and were armed
with lances, javelins, large shields and sometimes a bow.

Plate 4
Fig. 6

Despite the gradual Sarmatization of the Bosporans, the
neighbouring Sarmatian tribes were greatly influenced by, and
absorbed elements of, Bosporan culture during the revival of
Bosporan prosperity.

In the third century the Bosporans began to lose territory,
their trade declined and an economic crisis weakened the kingdom. The Bosporan army was unable to withstand the advancing
Goths, although by the end of the fourth century AD the Romans
still described it as an independent kingdom. The Hunnic
invasion finally put an end to its existence. Tanais, which had
been destroyed by the end of the fourth century AD, probably by
the Huns, suffered a similar fate.

THE 'TAMGA' SIGNS

Religion in the Bosporan Kingdom was strongly influenced by
Iranian ideas, thanks largely to contacts between the Bosporus
and the Kingdom of Pontus in the time of Mithridates VI
Eupator. After the conquest of the Persian Empire by Alexander
the Great, a movement developed in Iran, Asia Minor and the
neighbouring countries which attempted to synthesize the various
elements of Hellenistic and Iranian cultures and religions. This
movement extended as far as the neighbouring Sarmatian tribes.

An interesting expression of these new ideas is the appearance
in the Bosporan Kingdom in the first century AD of the so-
called 'tamga' signs. These religious symbols, which have been
incorrectly termed Sarmatian, have attracted the attention of many
archaeologists, and there is a conflict of opinion as to their precise
meaning and function. Some think they had a magical purpose,
others that they were marks of property. Their origin has often

Fig. 55

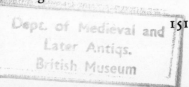

151

been sought in Iran, but here again no agreement has been reached.

The distribution of the tamgas (i.e. objects bearing these particular signs) in Eastern Europe is very limited, but indicates a Bosporan provenance. About two-thirds of all known 'Sarmatian' signs in Eastern Europe were found within Greek territory (the Bosporan Kingdom, Chersonesus, Olbia), and of the remainder about two-thirds within the Bosporan sphere of influence (the Crimea, the Kuban region). Only one-eighth of the total were found within Sarmatian territory proper, including four (out of more than 160) traced east of the Volga. The earliest tamgas, of the first century AD, are found exclusively within the Bosporan area, and those scattered throughout the Sarmatian steppes are all of the second and third centuries AD.

At this same date similar symbolic signs appear in the Central Asiatic territories of ancient Chorasmia and Fergana,[5] but at the present stage of research it is difficult to determine the connection between them and whether there is any genetic relationship.

The tamgas in Kerch and other Greek cities are carved or incised on tomb-stelae and in tomb-chambers; they also appear
Plate 37 as open-work on belt-buckles. The earliest follow a few established patterns, possibly representing monograms of Greek deities connected with both the cult of the sun and a belief in an after-life.[6] Later, the rigidity of design disappears, details are omitted and the monograms simplified; finally only a few characteristic features serve to recall the original patterns, though their ancestry is still recognizable.

Though the signs were adopted by the Siraces and the Aorsi, the Sarmatian peoples bordering on the Bosporan Kingdom, they were never adopted by the 'Eastern' (Transvolgan) Alans nor by the Goths who created the powerful Ostrogoth Kingdom in the Ukraine in the third century AD. They were unknown to the Iazyges and the Roxolani and other Sarmatian tribes who had left the steppe around the Bosporan Kingdom before the spread

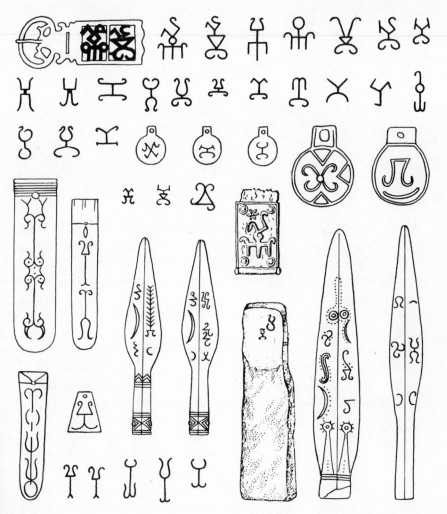

Fig. 55 Greek and Sarmatian tamgas of the first-third centuries AD: above, tamga signs on belt-buckles and strap-ends from the Bosporan kingdom, and on bronze mirrors mainly from the southern Ukraine; below, tamgas inlaid in silver on spear-heads from Poland; somewhat modified tamgas, some on strap-ends, of the fifth-sixth centuries AD from the Ukraine

Fig. 56   Survivals of tamgas in Polish heraldry of the eleventh-eighteenth centuries AD

of these symbols. Unlike the Bosporans, the Sarmatians did not associate the tamgas with a belief in life after death. Their tamgas are found in places clearly connected with worship, notably on the cliffs outside the entrance to several caves in the north-west Caucasus and the Crimean Mountains. On the steppe near Krivoy Rog on the River Ingulets, a huge stone block was found covered with tamga carvings. There are also tamgas on a large stone slab and a stone pillar found in Bessarabia and western Podolia. Otherwise tamgas appear most often on bronze mirrors, cauldrons and only exceptionally on buckles, doubtless because these were not in common use among the Sarmatians.

Tamgas of a more or less simplified kind are also found in late settlements further west, in Romania, west Podolia and as far as central and western Poland, evidently connected with the migration of some Sarmatian tribes.

The tamgas undoubtedly had religious or magical connotations: they were to guard the deceased in the after-life (the Bosporan belief), or to protect the owners of the objects marked with a tamga. After the conversion of the area to Christianity they lost their meaning and were replaced by the cross or the monogram of Christ. However they were not abandoned altogether,[7] and in some regions gradually acquired the character of marks of

Plate 38

Plates 39, 40

property or family crests: cattle and horses were branded with   *Fig. 56*
them by north Caucasian herdsmen until recent times.

THE NORTH PONTIC STEPPE

There are no extant written records of what happened after the
Alans had succeeded the Aorsi, but we know that several
tribes of the Aorsian stock retreated westwards to avoid the new
rule. Both Pliny and Ptolemy refer to a people called the 'Antae'
near the Sea of Azov west of the Don, who presumably were
identical with the 'An'ts'ai' of the Chinese *Annals* (see Chapter
IV). The Antae, who were probably the ruling tribe, have been
identified with the Aorsi. The name 'Antae' also appears on a
third-century stele at Panticapaeum, implying that at that time
they must have lived somewhere near the Bosporan Kingdom.

During the second century AD, the Western Alans, or another
group of the newly arrived Sarmatians, penetrated into the
Crimea and probably absorbed the Crimean 'Scythians', or
'Tauro-Scythians'.[8] However, no purely Sarmatian graves have
hitherto been found there, although burials in the cemetery of
Neapolis, the capital city, and other places yielded many grave
goods of a Sarmatian type. On the other hand, the presence of the
Satarches, a Sarmatian tribe, in the Crimea is reported in the
second century AD. They are said to have been fair, like the Alans,
and to have lived partly in caves, a fact which seems to indicate a
people of mixed blood, to which the aboriginal Crimeans
contributed. By the end of the third century AD the Goths and
other Teutonic tribes had invaded the Crimea and become its
masters.

SARMATIAN ARCHAEOLOGICAL REMAINS

Sarmatian archaeological remains in the North Pontic area have
not been sufficiently investigated. In the east, a number of richly
furnished, royal or princely, barrow graves, usually wrongly called
'hoards', have been found in the steppe between the Don and the

Fig. 57 Gold diadem set with semi-precious stones, from the Khokhlach-Novocherkassk barrow grave

Dnieper.[9] Presumably they are an indication of the Aorsi-Antae migration. They have been found in Voronezh, at Stanitsa Migulskaya, and elsewhere, but the best known is the Khokhlach barrow grave in the vicinity of Novocherkassk, known as the 'Novocherkassk hoard'. A woman, probably a tribal chief or queen, was buried there. The grave goods included at least thirteen gold objects, mostly decorated in the animal style and/or

Figs. 57, 58
Plates 41–44

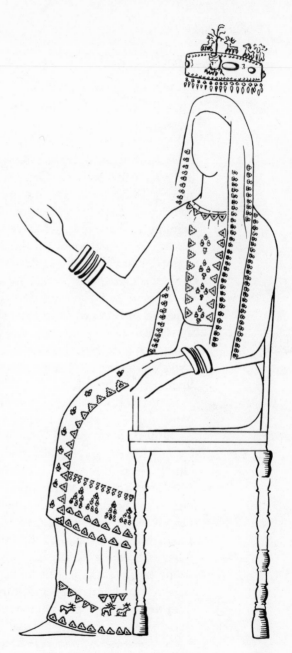

Fig. 58 Reconstruction of the dress of the Sarmatian queen buried in the Khokhlach-Novocherkassk barrow grave. The dress was decorated with small gold plaques (after a drawing in the Hermitage Museum, Leningrad)

studded with turquoise, amethyst, and coral, and richly ornamented bracelets, cases and jugs, a diadem and perfume-bottle.
One of the gold jugs has a characteristic Sarmatian zoomorphic
handle. There are hundreds of small gold plaques sewn on to
garments and head-dresses.

The culture of the Aorsian upper class was strongly influenced
by Transcaucasian (Iberian Kingdom) and Bosporan art and
included many Bosporan Greek elements. Features typical of the
ancient Pamir culture, inherited through the Prokhorovka
culture of the Early Sarmatian period, have also been distinguished,
pointing to the survival of ancient traditions within Sarmatian
society. Of special interest is the decorative style of some of the
objects, particularly the gold diadem from the Khokhlach-
Novocherkassk burial, where the stag figurines strikingly recall
the ancient 'Scythian' animal style which had long since disappeared in Europe. But the tradition probably still lingered on
somewhere in Siberia on the border of the steppe and forest-steppe
zones; its revival in Europe is evidently connected with the
arrival of a group of Sarmatians whose ancestral home must have
been east of the Urals.

A number of Sarmatian graves have been found in various
parts of the Ukraine, but their chronology has not been firmly
established. Their burial ritual, the type of grave (shaft, 'catacomb') and the grave goods (weapons, personal ornaments) are
almost identical with those in Sarmatian burials of the Middle
and Late Sarmatian periods in the lower Volga steppe; accordingly, the Ukrainian burials have all been attributed to the same
periods as the corresponding burials to the east. However, the
people buried in graves on the Ukrainian steppe were evidently
fugitives from the lower Volga area and the steppe-land further
to the east, who kept their former customs and only gradually
adopted new features. Their culture must, therefore, have differed
from that of the peoples who seized their country on the Volga.

Fig. 59   *Examples of Sarmatian niche, catacomb and other graves in mounds at*
Ust-Kamyanka on the lower Dnieper (after Makhno)

Fig. 59
Fig. 60

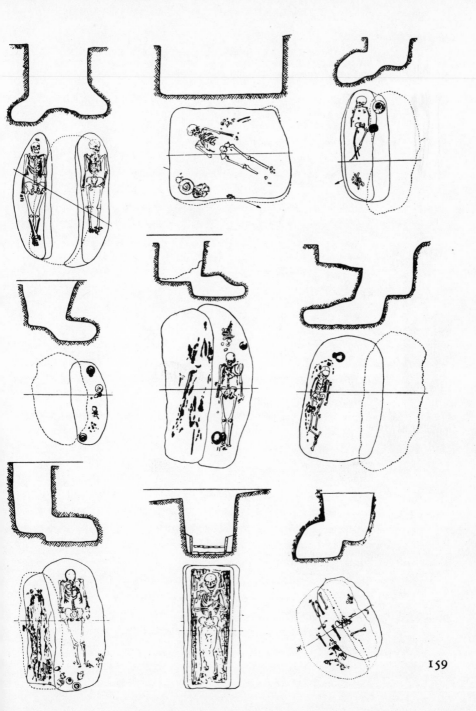

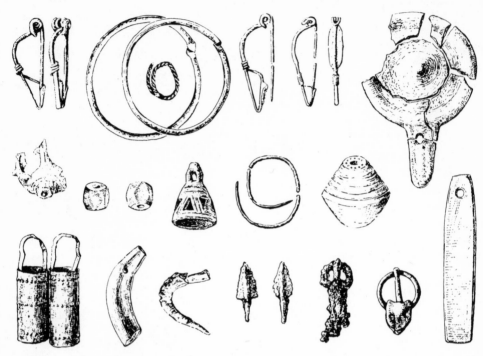

Fig. 60   Objects found in Late Sarmatian barrow graves at Ust-Kamyanka on the lower Dnieper (after Makhno)

Hence a time lag between these graves and the Late Sarmatian graves in the Volga steppe must be observed, and many Ukrainian burials of a Middle Sarmatian character must be dated as Late Sarmatian, from the mid-first century AD onwards. An early example of these is the richly furnished princely burial from Traiany near Balta.

Ukrainian graves attributable to the pre-Gothic late Sarmatian period have been found mainly in the lower Dnieper and Molochna regions.[10] These contained single Bosporan gold ornaments, ear-rings, paste beads, faience beads in the shape of

Fig. 61

Fig. 61   Egyptian faience talismans and amulets in the shape of scarabs, bunches of grapes, fists, human figurines, etc., found in North Pontic and Bosporan graves (after Piotrovskii)

scarabs, bunches of grapes or a fist, and white glass beads with golden threads and corals. Brooches, including the 'arlabest' type, are common, and among a variety of other objects kettles (cauldrons) are occasionally found.

Fig. 50

The Gothic invasion of the third century AD left a complex situation in the Ukraine. The Western Alans retreated west-wards leaving the country to the Goths, and consequently no Sarmatian remains of the third and fourth centuries have been found in the area west of the Dnieper. East of the Dnieper, between Poltava and Kursk as far as the Don, however, they have left many traces. This branch of Western Alans fell under the influence of the Eastern Alans of the Volga steppe and conse-quently their culture closely resembles that of the Late Sarmatian period on the Volga. A typical barrow-grave cemetery, dated partly to the second but mainly to the third century AD, has been excavated at Neshcheretove near Starobelsk, and several deformed skulls, a feature peculiar to the Eastern Alans on the Volga, were found.

Sarmatian remains within the steppe and forest-steppe zones between Poltava and Kursk overlap with the settlements and cemeteries of the Chernyakhiv culture, typical of the agricultural population of the Ukraine during the third and fourth centuries AD, which is regarded as East Slavonic. The Chernyakhiv group living within the territory of the Alans subsequently adopted many elements of their culture, while the Alanic group of that region exhibits several features derived from the Chernyakhiv culture. The cemetery of Kantemirivka (province of Poltava) reflects this development. Its graves are either flat, or under mounds; the burial ritual shows a syncretistic character, and the pottery is strongly influenced by that of the Chernyakhiv potters. The close contacts which obviously existed between these peoples, strengthened by intermarriages, ultimately resulted in the absorption of the Sarmatians by the people of the Chernyakhiv culture.[11]

In AD 214 great disturbances, caused by the movements of the 'barbarians', were reported in the North Pontic lands; the Goths are not named but it is widely accepted that they were the bar-barians in question. The date of a large number of hoards of Roman coins found in the Ukraine,[12] which were clearly hidden at a time of unrest, indicates that the Goths arrived on the middle Dnieper in about AD 200; from then on Sarmatian-Alan and Gothic history is interwoven. Gothic tradition, as transmitted by Jordanes, has it that the Goths came from the north and on reaching the country of 'Oium', somewhere on the middle Dnieper, had to fight the Spali, apparently a Sarmatian people. Sarmatian archaeological remains on the middle Dnieper (see Chapter IV) may accordingly be attributed to the Spali, and this also seems to be supported by the sudden downfall of this Sar-matian group in about AD 200, the time of the Gothic invasion. The Goths then advanced further southwards and ultimately they put an end to the Sarmatian domination in the Ukraine.

About AD 250 the Goths captured Olbia, which was then under Roman protection, thus sealing the city's fate: the minting of coins ceased and a gradual and final decline began; by the end of the sixth century, Olbia had ceased to exist. The Goths also put an end to the Tauro-Scythian Kingdom; the Bosporan Kingdom, still nominally under Roman rule, was likewise sub-dued. In AD 332, the last Bosporan coins were minted; the last Bosporan King, Rheskuporis IV, died in AD 361/2. In the fourth century the Dniester formed the western boundary of the Gothic (Ostrogothic) Empire in the Ukraine; in the east it did not extend beyond the Dnieper except for a narrow strip on the Sea of Azov up to the Don estuary. Further north the steppe-land between the Don and the Dnieper was occupied by the Alans.

As a result of their conquest of the steppe and their seizure of the Bosporan Kingdom, the culture of the Ostrogoths acquired many Sarmatian features. Bosporan workshops began to supply the new customers, adapting the old Sarmato-Bosporan jewellery patterns to their new masters' taste, and adding features introduced by the newcomers. The resulting new 'Gothic' art later spread over the whole of Central and Western Europe, carried and disseminated by the Goths and other peoples including the Sarmatian Alans, retreating before the Huns.

THE FUGITIVE SARMATIANS IN THE WEST

The situation in the western division of the North Pontic area during the later third and fourth century AD is very confused. No Sarmatian remains of this period have been found between the Dnieper and the Dniester. The Western Alans had probably departed under pressure from the Goths, migrating either southwards and/or westwards. The archaeological evidence indicates that some of them arrived in east Walachia, but most settled in the northern half of Bessarabia and the adjoining part of Moldavia on the other side of the River Pruth. There the Alans must have subjugated the native population of Getic ancestry, since the country is referred to by contemporary writers as 'Alania', and the Pruth as the 'Alan river' (*Alanus fluvius*), although for a time they may have been under Gothic suzerainty. A number of place-names containing the root 'Yas', including the capital city of Moldavia, Iaşi, suggest they were a branch of the Western Alans, the Aorsi, Iasi, or Ptolemy's Asaioi. We may further identify them with the Antae whose presence in that region is recorded in the fourth century AD, and who remained there until the sixth century AD, although by that date through assimilation they were known as a Slavonic, not Sarmatian, people.

The north-western boundary of the Bessarabian group of the Sarmatians (Alans, Antae) has not been established. It may have included the southern part of western Podolia: a Sarmatian bronze mirror (Sapohów) and stone slab with tamga signs engraved on it (Trembowla) were found there. Topo-

Fig. 62

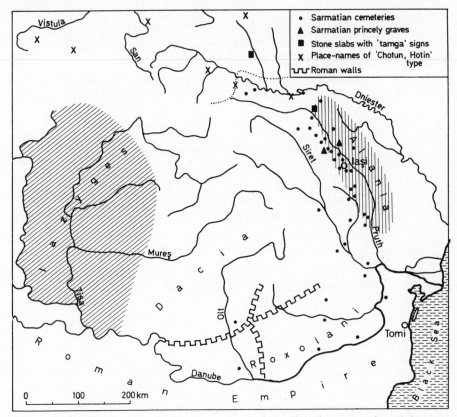

Fig. 62   Sites from the Late Sarmatian period in the basin of the lower Danube and the upper Dniester, third-fifth centuries AD

graphical names of Alanic origin appear in western Podolia, but also further to the west and north; the names of several ancient strongholds (earthworks) north-west of the Bessarabian centre are of Alanic origin, among them Bessarabian Hotin on the Dniester, Chocin near Kałusz in the Carpathian foothills, Chotyniec on the San north of Przemyśl. They also appear in several places in central Poland, north Bohemia, south Slovakia and east Germany. However, the western names may have

Fig. 71

originated at a later date, being connected with the Sarmatian Western (White) Croats (see Chapter VI).

In AD 375, according to Jordanes, the Antae rebelled against their Gothic overlords, but were conquered by Vinitarius (Vitmir), King of the Ostrogoths, who crucified their King Boz (Buz) and no less than 70 chieftains. This number implies that the Antae must have been a numerous people.

SARMATIAN TRACES IN POLAND

Fig. 55

Archaeological evidence suggests that the Western Alans, possibly the Antae, expanded into modern Poland, where they appear as an isolated off-shoot.[13] In the first centuries AD, a Slavonic people of the Przeworsk culture had occupied Poland, but it underwent considerable changes at the beginning of the third century AD. Wheel-turned pottery of the Pontic (Dacian) type suddenly appears together with characteristic Sarmatian tendrilled brooches 'with the foot turned over', and iron spear-heads with silver inlaid tamga signs. A number of richly furnished graves, a feature hitherto unknown in the Przeworsk culture, were evidently the tombs of rulers, presumably the country's con-querors. Some of the most notable are at Zakrzów (Sacrau) in Silesia where the grave goods include objects of North Pontic origin and Sarmatian type belt-buckles.

What caused this change? The evidence (especially the tamgas) points to the Antae from Bessarabia, or perhaps another West Alanic, Aorsian, tribe which had absorbed elements of Bosporan culture during its sojourn in the North Pontic steppe throughout the first and second centuries AD. The presence of Sarmatians in Poland is mentioned in the fifth century Lango-bardian Chronicle (*Origo Gentis Langobardorum*) which, in des-cribing the journey of the Langobards from their original home on the lower Elbe to Lower Austria, says that they were forced to fight their way through the 'Anthaib', the land of the Antae. This has been variously interpreted but the most likely explanation is that of F. Dvornik to the effect that the Antae territory included Silesia and Lesser Poland, through which the Lango' bards passed on their way south.

The kingdom of the Alanic Antae in Poland was, however, short'lived and in the fifth century AD they were subdued by the Huns from Hungary. Nevertheless ancient Sarmatian traditions survived in Poland for a long time. A belief in the Sarmatian origin of Poland was widespread for centuries among the Polish nobility. Tamga signs appear on eleventh'century coins, and the most striking survival is in Polish heraldry, where ancient tam' gas appear in stylized form as crescents, arrows, horseshoes, etc.

Fig. 56

THE ROXOLANI ON THE DANUBE

We turn now to the Roxolani, one of the first two Sarmatian peoples to retreat from the North Pontic area. By the middle of the first century AD, the Roxolani were compelled to move west of the Dnieper. Some of their tribes settled between the Dnieper and the Danube delta (ousting the Iazyges who had been there before them), but the majority went further south and, in AD 62, their presence was reported in the plains of southern Romania.

We have already followed the movements of the Roxolani on the Danube up to the middle of the first century AD. In the winter of AD 69 they again invaded Moesia and annihilated the Legio III Gallica, but another Roman army soon took them by surprise and severely punished them. In AD 85–86 they attacked Moesia yet again, and in Trajan's wars against the Dacians fought on the Dacian side; the Iazyges, then in the Hungarian Plain, fought on the side of the Romans. When Trajan celebrated his triumph in AD 107, captive Roxolani, as well as Dacians, were led through the streets of Rome; a fugitive detachment of Roxolanian heavy cavalry clad in scale armour is depicted on Trajan's Column.

Plate 4

After the Dacian wars the Roxolani were given a subsidy as long as they kept away from Roman frontiers, but in AD 117 this was discontinued. Another war ensued which was quelled by Hadrian, Trajan's successor; the subsidy was renewed and the King of the Roxolani became a Roman vassal in AD 118. This may have been the P. Aelius Rasparaganus, *Rex Roxolanorum*, whose name is mentioned on two inscriptions in Pula (Pola) in Istria, Yugoslavia. The Roxolani were allowed to make contact —across the Roman province of Dacia—with their kindred, the Iazyges in Banat and the Hungarian Plain.

The peace lasted until AD 260 when the Goths invaded Dacia. Soon afterwards, in AD 271, Dacia was abandoned by the Romans. The arrival of the Goths had a marked impact on the Roxolani. During the third and fourth centuries AD raids by Sarmatians into Roman territory south of the Danube were undertaken jointly with the Goths, especially during the reign of Gallienus (AD 253–268), but the identity of the Sarmatian tribes taking part is uncertain. Those depicted on the Arch of Galerius at Salonica (AD 297), for example, could be the Roxolani, but they could equally well be Western Alans.

In AD 331, the Goths and Taifales tried to oust the Roxolani from Muntenia (southern Romania), and some of them had to move westwards, south of the country occupied by the Iazyges, where 'diagonal' graves dating from this period have been found. In AD 377 the remaining Roxolani abandoned the Romanian plain under pressure from the Ostrogoths who, in turn, were retreating before the Huns. Some Roxolani sought refuge in Roman Moesia; others retreated to the west and joined their kin in Hungary.

SARMATIAN SITES IN MOLDAVIA AND BESSARABIA

Over thirty sites have been found in Romania east of the Carpathians containing archaeological remains of several distinct groups of Sarmatians.[14]

Fig. 63

In the plain of eastern Walachia and southern Moldavia Sarmatian graves appear either isolated or in groups. Their equipment includes beads, brooches, small bronze mirrors with a

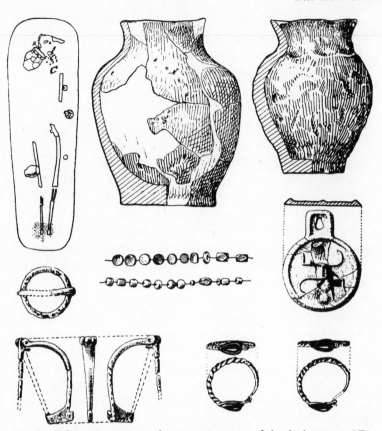

Fig. 63   Plan and equipment of a Sarmatian grave of the third century AD from the cemetery at Tîrgișor in southern Romania; fifty per cent of the skulls excavated at that cemetery were deformed (after Diaconu)

perforated grip, some with the tamga decoration, sometimes iron swords, and one or two clay vessels. All are typical of the early part of the Late Sarmatian period in the Ukraine: grave goods of the same type, dating from the second and early third centuries AD and attributable to the Western Alans, have been excavated on the Molochna. Possibly, therefore, the Romanian burials, which have been ascribed to the Roxolani, belong rather to the Western Alans, who may have mingled with the Roxolani upon reaching the area and then absorbed them. The presence of deformed skulls in a few of the graves seems to bear this out.

Sarmatian remains have also been found in settlements and cemeteries—where they took the form mainly of cremations in urns—of the Chilia-Poieneşti culture, extending over the sub-Carpathian foothills of southern Moldavia and Walachia; the peoples in question were probably the indigenous Daco-Getae, or possibly the Carpi. Among grave goods typical of the Sarmatian culture are beads, bronze mirrors, often broken during the funeral in accordance with Sarmatian practice, small bronze 'bells', etc. The cremation urns, non-Sarmatian wheel-turned ware with zoomorphic handles closely resembling those of Sarmatian vessels in the lower Volga and the north-west Caucasus area, are particularly interesting. The cemeteries were mostly in use during the third century AD, but some were set up in the second century and lasted into the fourth century AD. The character and number of these remains suggest that the Sarmatians formed a relatively large proportion of the population, although they were subsequently assimilated by the indigenous element.

There is also a rather high proportion of Sarmatian remains in a number of indigenous settlements in northern Moldavia and Bessarabia; and a few isolated Sarmatian graves have been found in this area as well. The settlements and cemeteries belong to the local branch of the Ukrainian Chernyakhiv culture, known in its localized form as the Sintana-de-Mureş, which includes many elements of the preceding local Daco-Getan culture. The grave goods are characteristic of the early stage of the Late Sarmatian period in the steppe east of the Dnieper: bronze rings and other personal ornaments, necklaces of glass or carnelian beads, bronze mirrors some with the tamga decoration, occasionally an iron sword, in one instance a Roman imported glass beaker. One of the skeletons at Mitoc was sprinkled with a white substance (chalk?) in the manner typical of the Early and Middle Sarmatian period in the east, and the marks made by a bronze diadem were visible on the skull. To this group of remains belongs also a stone slab with engraved tamgas found in northern Bessarabia at Teţcani.

A branch of the Sarmatians, presumably the Western Alani (Aorsi, Asi), had evidently settled in northern Moldavia and the adjoining part of Bessarabia by the end of the second century AD; the tamga signs indicate that this group originated on the northwestern shores of the Sea of Azov. They seem to have been joined later by small groups of Eastern Alans, their eastern kinsmen, who introduced the cranial deformation recorded in some Sarmatian graves in Romania.

THE IAZYGES IN HUNGARY: THE EARLY PERIOD

The Iazyges were among the earliest of the Sarmatians to cross the Don and start the exodus from the lower Volga steppes. In the Middle Sarmatian period they lived somewhere in the Dniester steppe, but their presence was also felt further south, on the Danube and in Dobruja, which was then part of the Roman Empire. Probably about AD 20–30 they moved further west before the advancing Roxolani, and found themselves in the north of the Hungarian Plain and eastern Slovakia. Their route has not been established; some scholars think that they crossed the Carpathians from the Bucovina to the upper Tisa valley, while others think they followed the Danube valley round the Carpathians. In their new country they partly displaced, but mostly subdued, the CeltoDacian occupants. Tacitus mentions the Cotini and Orsi as indigenous tribes northeast of Budapest who paid tribute to them. The archaeological evidence shows that the native population managed to preserve its identity at least until the end of the third century AD, and their influence on the newcomers is illustrated by a series of objects, brooches and arm-rings, mostly of the La Tène type, found in early Sarmatian graves.

The presence of the Iazyges in the Hungarian Plain influenced the geographical concepts of the period. Agrippa's map (*c.* AD 12) mentions the Dacians as the eastern neighbours of the Teutonic tribes, in accordance with the situation on the northern frontier of the Empire during his time, when Dacian tribes lived in northern Hungary and eastern Slovakia east of the Germanic

Fig. 64

Suevi. Thirty years later, however, *c.* AD 44, Pomponius Mela introduced the term 'Sarmatia' for the country east of 'Germania'. Thus his work, written some twenty years after the Iazyges' invasion of the Hungarian Plain, recognizes the situation obtain-ing in the area, even though it retains the old name 'Scythia' for the Pontic lands in which Sarmatians had replaced the Scythians several centuries earlier.

In his description of north-west Europe, Pomponius Mela used data obtained by a Roman naval expedition which in AD 5 sailed as far as Jutland. Of all the Germanic tribes in the area, only one, the Hermiones, lived east of the Elbe, but Pomponius Mela did not know of the non-Germanic, presumably proto-Slavonic, tribes who were their neighbours. It seems he assumed that they were Sarmatians—as was the case along the Roman frontier in Hungary—and accordingly applied the name 'Sar-matia' to the whole territory inhabited by non-Germanic tribes north of the Danube and east of the Elbe.

The use of the name 'Sarmatia' to cover the non-Germanic countries of Central Europe persisted, although the dividing line between Germania and Sarmatia changed. Ptolemy and his successors shifted it to the Vistula and extended Sarmatia to include the whole of Eastern Europe as well as Central Europe.

The Iazyges, whom the Romans always called 'the Sarmatians', remained for over 450 years in the Hungarian Plain and, since they were isolated from their kin in the North Pontic area, their history has little in common with that of other Sarmatian peoples

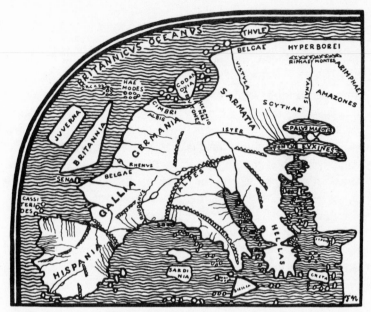

Fig. 64   Map of Europe according to the description of Pomponius Mela, about AD 44 (after Nansen and Łowmiański)

who remained in the east. The main links were groups of the Roxolani and Alans who, in retreating west after various major disturbances in the Ukraine, crossed the Carpathians and joined them. The newcomers usually disturbed the status quo and upset relations with neighbouring peoples, particularly the Roman Empire, bringing grave consequences upon themselves and the local Sarmatian Iazyges.

The history of the Sarmatians in Hungary may be divided into three periods:[15] Early (*c.* AD 20–160), Middle (160–260) and Late (260–430). During the Early period the Iazyges were evidently on good terms with the Romans; they apparently had a treaty with them under which they served as auxiliaries. In AD 50 an Iazygian cavalry detachment fought alongside Vannius, King of the Suevi and a vassal of the Roman Empire. Although bordering on Roman Pannonia, the Iazyges never entered the province; their main strength was concentrated against the Dacians and they fought against them as allies of Rome in Trajan's Dacian wars of AD 85–88 and 101. However, in AD 92, after penetrating south to the Danube at the expense of the Dacians, they ravaged Roman Moesia. In AD 105 the country was retaken by Decebalus, King of the Dacians, but a year later Dacia was conquered by the Romans. In AD 117–119, Hadrian had a hard fight when the Iazyges attacked Roman Dacia (Transylvania) from the west, and the Roxolani attacked it from the east (from Walachia). The Sarmatians were repulsed and a treaty concluded which led to a peace lasting for fifty years.

Judging by their earliest remains, the Iazyges were not a numerous people; they were divided into three shifting territorial units. Their graves are flat and are grouped together in large cemeteries. They are poorly furnished: clay vessels, sometimes an iron knife, beads, occasionally a brooch, exceptionally a short iron sword with a ring instead of a pommel, of a type taken over from the Prokhorovka culture of the Early Sarmatian period. In a few graves, probably the earliest, small decorative gold plates of various shapes sewn on to garments of a North Pontic type, were found. As there are no North Pontic objects in later graves, it must be assumed that connections were severed with countries east of the Carpathians.

Plates 48, 49

THE MIDDLE SARMATIAN PERIOD IN HUNGARY

A new phase opened when the Sarmatians broke the peace to participate in the Marcomanian Wars (AD 166–172, 177–180) as one of Rome's chief adversaries. Their efforts were now directed mainly westwards, against Pannonia, and only one Sarmatian incursion into Transylvania is recorded (AD 167), when the Dacian gold mines were temporarily abandoned by the Romans.

In AD 169 the Sarmatians crossed the Danube and invaded Pannonia, only to be severely trounced by Marcus Aurelius, an encounter on the frozen Danube vividly described by Dio

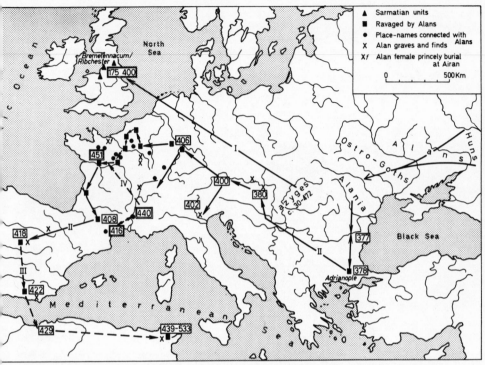

Fig. 65 The Sarmatians (Iazyges and Alans) in western Europe. Recorded dates are indicated in the frames. I A detachment of 5,000 Iazygian cavalry transferred by Marcus Aurelius to England, after their defeat in AD 175. II Itinerary of a detachment of Alans retreating before the Huns. III Final section of their itinerary: after being routed by the Visigoths, the Alans joined and mingled with the Vandals. IV Recorded movements of another Alanic detachment in the service of the Romans in France. (Place-names associated with the Alans: Alençon-Orne; Alaigne-Aude; Allain-aux-Boefs; Allaines; Allainville-en-Drouais; Alaincourt; Allan)

Cassius. It was not until AD 175 that peace was concluded, when Marcus took the title 'Sarmaticus' and his victories were cele- brated in the Imperial coinage. Harsh terms were imposed on the Sarmatians: they were required to live at a distance from the Danube and to contribute 8,000 cavalrymen to the Roman army, 5,500 of whom were sent to Britain. These were stationed on the northern border in units of 500, and four sites bearing traces

Plate 45

Fig. 65

Fig. 66   Sarmatian beads from the Roman fort at Chesters, Hadrian's wall, where a detachment of Sarmatians was posted. Their only parallels are beads from Sarmatian graves in Hungary

of them have ṣo far been discovered.[16] In the Roman fort at Chesters on Hadrian's wall an eye-shield, probably Sarmatian, from a cataphract horse was found, and a number of beads typical of the Hungarian Sarmatians. A Sarmatian unit at the fort of Morbium is mentioned in *Notitia Dignitorum*, and in the ancient fort of Bremetennacum at Ribchester near Lancaster, were found inscriptions referring to a Sarmatian cavalry unit 500 strong. Finally, a funeral stele with a carving in relief representing a Sarmatian officer was recovered from the camp at Chester.

Nothing is known of the fate of these men, but the majority never returned to their homeland. A settlement of veterans was established at Bremetennacum; it never became a real town, but was still in existence in the early fifth century AD.

In Dacia war broke out again after only two years' peace, and the Iazyges won some mitigation of the previous terms. They were allowed to sail the Danube in their own boats in order to communicate with the Roxolani, who lived in the Romanian plain east of Dacia, and were their source of supply for the beads and

Fig. 66

Plate 46

other commodities of eastern origin which constitute their usual grave goods.

Hostilities with the Romans continued intermittently. We hear of the Emperor Maximus Thrax assuming the title 'Sar/maticus Maximus' after a campaign against the Iazyges in AD 236–238; we hear of Iazyges raiding Dacia in 248–250, and Pannonia in 254 in conjunction with the Quades.

The archaeological remains of the Hungarian Middle Sar/matian period are more numerous and widespread and differ in many respects from those of the Early period, although they still reflect a nomadic, pastoral way of life. The grave goods consisted of clay vessels, brooches and exceptionally short iron swords mainly with a pommel, seldom with a ring (in male graves) or a whorl or bronze mirror (in female burials). One new feature is the so/called 'herdsmen's bag'—a collection of items comprising an iron knife, iron awl, fire/steel and flint, and sometimes a whetstone.

Some richly furnished barrow graves, known as the 'Nagyhegy group' scattered throughout Iazygian territory, though few in number, are of interest. They evidently belonged to the ruling class and differ from other graves in their burial ritual and grave goods. Weapons are common and a horse was often buried with its master. Many of the objects are of eastern origin: Indian beads and small thin North Pontic gold and bronze plates sewn on to garments. A notable example was discovered at Szil in the centre of Roman Pannonia, possibly the grave of a Sarmatian prince who fell in battle during a raid in the second century AD.

An increase in the number of graves of the Hungarian Middle Sarmatian period, of objects of Pontic origin, of vessels with zoomorphic handles typical of the lower Volga and Kuban Sarmatians (Alans), and similar eastern features, indicate the arrival of a fresh wave of Sarmatians. It is, however, difficult to establish their identity. They may have been a branch of the Roxolani, or perhaps a group of Western Alans, driven west/

Plate 47

Plate 51

Fig. 67

wards by events in the late first and second centuries AD. Upon entering the Hungarian Plain, the newcomers seem to have overcome the Iazyges, but opinions vary as to whether they arrived in Hungary after the Marcomanian Wars, i.e. after AD 180, or before them, i.e. before AD 166—the outbreak of the wars being a result of their arrival.

THE LATE SARMATIAN PERIOD IN HUNGARY

By the middle of the third century AD the final decline of the Hungarian Sarmatians marks the beginning of the Late Sarmatian period. The Gepidae, an aggressive Teutonic people, settled to the north of them; in AD 260 the Goths entered Dacia, which the Romans could no longer defend, and in AD 271 established the powerful Visigothic Kingdom. Despite this danger on their eastern border, the Sarmatians, aided by the Quades, continued raids into Pannonia (the most destructive was in AD 282–283) until, between AD 290 and 313, eight successive Roman expeditions raided and devastated Iazygian territory, the Emperor Galerius Maximus and his successors, Constantine and Licinius, subsequently taking the title 'Sarmaticus'.

These Roman punitive expeditions weakened, but did not break, the Sarmatians. But they could not have resisted the Visigoths who attacked them in AD 321, before going on to invade Pannonia, had not the campaign ended in victory for Constantine in AD 322: the Gothic king was slain, and the Sarmatians saved.

The Sarmatians' renewed activity, to which the Romans reacted so violently, seems to have been connected with internal changes, most probably caused by a new wave of immigrants from the east. The contents of their graves seem to indicate three distinct social strata: a lower class, possibly descendants of the indigenous conquered Dacians, mainly engaged in agriculture, who did not lose their identity; a middle class, perhaps the first Iazygian wave, which absorbed subsequent waves of new

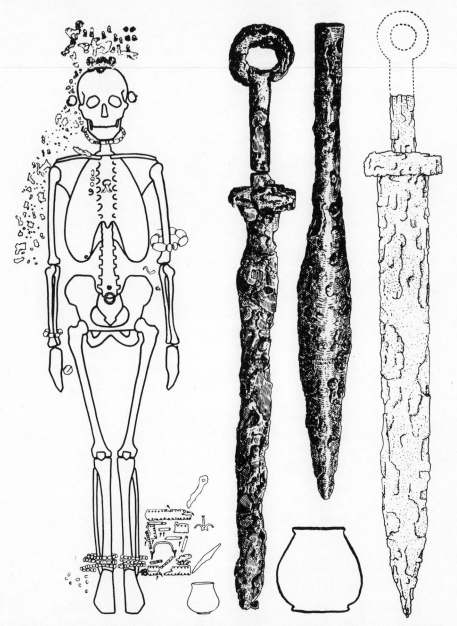

Fig. 67   Plan of a Sarmatian burial at Szentes-Nagyhegy, early third century AD (the Middle
Sarmatian period in Hungary); weapons and a vase from burials of the same period at Szil and
Kiskunfélegyháza in Hungary (after Párducz)

comers from the east; and the ruling upper class, possibly third, century newcomers whose tombs are the few barrow graves concentrated mainly in the north, east of the Tisa.

Naturally the archaeological remains of the three groups differ to some extent. The graves of the first, the 'Bajmok-Mórohalom' group are flat, and possess no weapons. The cemeteries of the second, the 'Kiszombór-Ernöháza' group, consist of up to thirty flat burials of pure Sarmatians in wooden coffins, containing

Plate 50   'herdsmen's bags', personal ornaments and occasionally an iron sword and Roman coins; in one grave a long double-edged iron sword typical of the Roxolani was found. The remains of the third group consist exclusively of barrow graves whose burial ritual and equipment are identical with the flat graves of the second group but which, unlike these, are furnished with

Plate 52   weapons, horses and fine Pontic jewellery, especially the ten-drilled fibulae of the type 'with the foot turned over'. The proximity of the Goths and Gepidae led to the adoption of a few objects characteristic of these peoples. One particularly interesting barrow grave, dating from about AD 300, was found at Herpály, on the eastern fringe of Iazygian territory, where a Sarmatian warrior, evidently belonging to the upper class, was buried with his horse. The grave contained characteristic Sarmatian beads and

Plate 53   a fine Teutonic-type shield-boss covered with a gold-plated silver sheet decorated in the Pontic style.

The members of the third group were probably descended from the ruling class of the preceding Middle Sarmatian period. But it seems that the newcomers were the decisive and important element. The old name 'Iazyges' does not appear in contemporary written records, being replaced by the more general term 'Sarmatians'. Obviously, the ancient tribal name was dropped because the newcomers, who belonged to a different tribe, had gained the upper hand; their identity has not yet been established. The imported Pontic objects and connections suggest a North Pontic origin for the newcomers; they were probably Alans from the steppe west of the Dniester retreating westwards before the invading Goths.

The final stage of the Hungarian Late Sarmatian period began about AD 332, when a disastrous civil war broke out. The vassal tribe the 'Sarmatae Limigantes' rose against their masters, the 'Sarmatae Ardagarantes', also called 'Sarmatae Libri'. Over 100,000 barbarians were said to have participated in the fighting, which went badly for the Ardagarantes. Some fled to the Quades and Goths, but the majority took refuge in Roman territory and were given land in Pannonia or present-day Yugoslav Vojvodina.

In AD 355 and 357, the Limigantes invaded and plundered Upper Moesia and Lower Pannonia but were defeated by the Emperor Constantius in 358. The Ardagarantes were then restored by the Romans to their former country, and a native prince, Zizais, installed as their king. The following year, however, discontented with their new home, they asked permission to settle within the limits of the Empire, and then attempted to avenge their loss of territory by a treacherous onslaught on the Emperor. He escaped and the whole tribe was massacred by the Romans.

Sarmatian incursions into Pannonia are reported again in AD 364, 374 and 378, when they were repulsed by the Emperor Theodosius. In AD 384, Theodosius triumphed over the Sarmatians jointly with his son Arcadius and his co-Emperor Valentinianus II.

The end of the period has usually been put at about AD 430, the time of the Huns' seizure of the country; but the Sarmatians in Hungary are still mentioned in written records nearly fifty years later.

Archaeological research provides supplementary data on the latest Sarmatian period in Hungary. The three Late Sarmatian groups are still distinguishable although their burial equipment has changed. The remains appear approximately within the same territory as before but they are considerably fewer. It is not possible to apportion them to the Limigantes and Ardagarantes.

The most marked difference occurs in the Tápé-Malajdok group, which succeeded the Kiszombór-Ernöháza group. New types of fibulae, buckles and beads are found along with examples characteristic of the preceding period. But the most significant innovation is the appearance of weapons in the graves. The newly introduced grave goods mentioned above are also found in the other two groups, and these changes suggest the arrival of new ethnic elements and an intermingling with the local Sarmatians, although the latter continued the traditions of the preceding period.

Now for the first time barrow graves appear in the south, in the area between the Danube and the Tisa, where only a few Sarmatian remains from the preceding period have been found. They are much larger than those investigated in the north of the Hungarian Plain, although the grave goods are almost identical. Several 'diagonal' graves were discovered under mounds, presumably chieftains' burials. The group is attributable to a section of the Roxolani who under pressure from the Visigoths abandoned Walachia and joined their kindred people in the south of the Hungarian Plain.

CHAPTER VI

Epilogue

THE HUNNIC INVASION

THE GOTHIC INVASION of the Ukraine *c.* AD 200 ended Iranian supremacy in South-Eastern Europe which had lasted well over a millennium. Ostrogothic rule brought nearly two centuries of prosperity to the region and the Sarmatian and Gothic cultures each had an influence on the other.

The Ostrogothic empire was not destined to last any longer than the rule of its predecessors in the North Pontic area, where the Scythians and Sarmatian tribes had followed each other in consecutive periods lasting some two hundred years.

About AD 355 the Huns entered Europe and swarmed across the lower Volga and Don steppe. Their advance marks the beginning of a new era, the era of Turcoman supremacy in Eastern Europe, which lasted for about eight centuries. The Huns had already seized the ancient homelands of the Sarmatians in Asia during the second and third centuries AD, and now took possession of the last of their original territories. Some of the Eastern Alans who lived there retreated westwards, others sought refuge in the Caucasus, but most were caught up with the Huns and subsequently drawn into Central Europe. The Huns' irresistible impetus continued, and in AD 375 they broke the mighty Ostrogoth Kingdom.

The savage onslaught of the Huns brought disaster to the whole North Pontic area. The flourishing Bosporan towns were ravaged, some (e.g. Tanais) were completely destroyed and never rebuilt. The Cherniakhiv people,[1] the native population of the Ukraine under Gothic rule, also suffered. Their settlements were burned down, and the majority of them seem to have fled south into Romania or crossed the Carpathians to settle in Transylvania.[2]

As a result of the last great Sarmatian-Alanic migratory movement that had begun after the Hunnic disaster, individual tribes had branched off into almost every country from the Volga to Spain, and in the east as far as China. This was virtually the end of the Sarmatians as a distinct people. Split into smaller and smaller units in many isolated regions, they had little chance of maintaining their national identity, and were doomed to be absorbed either by successive conquerors or else by the subject peoples in the countries to which they had retreated.

Much the same was to be the lot of the Ostrogoths. After their defeat, some Ostrogoths remained in the Crimea and, along with splinter groups of the Alans, acknowledged Hunnic supremacy. But the majority migrated westwards, as did Visigoths from the region south of the Dniester and some groups of Western Alans. The Emperor Valens permitted them all to cross the Danube and settle within the Roman Empire. Soon, however, conflict with Roman officials caused them to rebel and, in the famous battle of Adrianople that followed in AD 378, the Roman army was crushed by the united Goths and Alans, whose cavalry played a decisive role, and Valens himself was killed. Thereby they set in

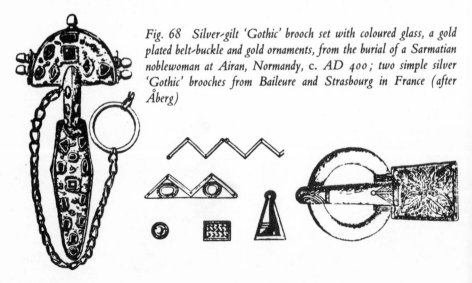

Fig. 68   Silver-gilt 'Gothic' brooch set with coloured glass, a gold plated belt-buckle and gold ornaments, from the burial of a Sarmatian noblewoman at Airan, Normandy, c. AD 400; two simple silver 'Gothic' brooches from Baileure and Strasbourg in France (after Åberg)

motion the train of events that culminated in the sack of Rome by the Ostrogoths in 410, and marked the end of the ancient order in Europe.

THE ALANS IN CENTRAL AND WESTERN EUROPE

The fate of the Alans who retreated westwards before the Huns is complicated, and tracing all their groups in the countries of their refuge is not an easy task. Prior to the Hunnic invasion, in the North Pontic area west of the Dnieper, Alans and Goths had already adopted some of each other's ornaments and other articles. This meant that the material culture of both peoples became similar, so that Alanic burials are often hard to distin-guish from those of the Goths. Furthermore, the Alans being cut off from their steppe homeland, their culture underwent con-siderable changes in their new environment.

However, a few special objects found in ancient burials may serve as an indication of the Sarmatian-Alanic origin of the person buried. Among these are small bronze mirrors and small gold plates of characteristic design sewn on to garments. The *Fig. 68* Alans also adopted from the Goths the 'Gothic plate brooches',

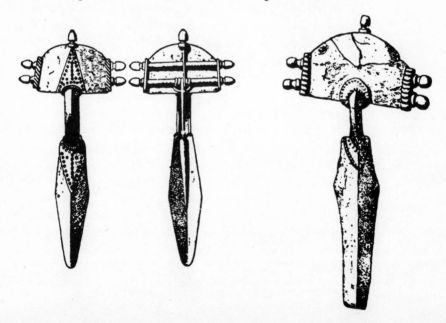

and after the Hunnic invasion, they contributed—jointly with the Ostrogoths—to their dissemination, in their retreat westwards over Central and Western Europe as far as France and Spain,[3] and to the adoption of a more or less modified form of the 'Gothic plate brooch' by several Teutonic peoples.

Most 'Gothic plate brooches' have been attributed to the Goths, even those found in areas of northern France where the presence of neither Ostrogoths nor Visigoths has been recorded, and despite the fact that the finds ante-date the arrival of the Goths in France. The western 'Gothic' brooches, and many of the same type found in a series of sites in central Europe, may be attributed to groups of Western Alans who retreated before the advancing Huns.

The few archaeological remains, but above all the brief mentions scattered in the written records of the Migration and early Mediaeval periods, give some insight into the Alanic *Fig. 65* dispersal. Thus the story of one group can be traced in detail. In AD 377 this group, which was quite large, crossed the Danube and, together with a group of Huns, joined the Visigoths and Ostrogoths in ravaging Roman territory in the Balkans.

In AD 380, with the Ostrogoths and the Hunnic detachment, these Alans drove northwards and settled in Pannonia. Twenty years later they joined the Vandals and crossed into Noricum, the adjoining province to the north-west. Here they were opposed by the Romans under Stilicho, who granted them land in return for pledges of service. In 402–405 they fought in the Roman army against the Visigoths.

In AD 406, however, they set out to invade Gaul with the Vandals and Suevi. Under their King Respendial they crossed the Rhine near Mainz and defeated the Franks. Some of the Alans, under King Goar, then offered their services to Rome, but the majority, under Respendial, and the two allied Teutonic peoples began a 'tour de France', devastating the countryside and cities. Their route was unopposed and led from Mainz through Trèves

(Trier), Rheims, Arras, Amiens, and then Paris, Orleans, Tour, Bordeaux and Toulouse. In 408, after terrorizing Gaul for two years, the Alans went to Spain and with their allies ravaged the whole peninsula, finally settling in Lusitania, modern Portugal and Spain west of Madrid.

In 418 the Alans were routed by the Visigoths, who had been enlisted by the Roman Emperor for a drive against the 'barbarians'. Addac, King of the Alans, was killed and the remnants of the people fled to Galicia where they joined the Vandals. Gunderich, King of the Vandals, assumed the title *Rex Vandalorum et Alanorum*, which was retained by his successors until the end of the Vandal Kingdom in AD 533.

Thus ended the independent existence of this branch of the Alans. In the forty years since they left their original steppe/lands, they had crossed a whole continent. Even now their wanderings were not ended: in 422, together with the Vandals, they left Galicia for southern Spain, and in 429 crossed into Africa, where they were gradually absorbed by the Vandals.

Another group of Alans also reached France. Under King Goar, they were at different times allied with the Visigoths and the Romans; they are probably the Alans who are reported at Narbonne in 416 and later at Orleans. They seem not to have resisted the Huns in 451 but in 452 they were subjugated by the Visigoths. We hear of other Alanic kings (Beogus *Rex Alanorum* in 464; Eochar *ferrocissimus Alanorum rex* in 440) taking part in the confused struggles which ushered in the Dark Ages. The Alans ultimately merged with the indigenous population of France, but over thirty French place/names connected with 'Sarmatians' or 'Alans', among them the name of the town Alençon, bear witness to their presence. The Beaucerons in the region of Orleans may possibly be descended from them.[4]

A few archaeological remains attributable to wandering groups of Sarmatians/Alans have been found west of Hungary.[5] They include the richly furnished graves at Laa/an/der/Thaye and Untersiebenbrunnen near Vienna, and Airan in Normandy, all dated to AD *c*. 400. 'Gothic' silver plate brooches (the two examples from Airan are gold plated, and set with coloured stones), ornaments of various types and small bronze mirrors were among their grave goods. Dating from the same period— the early fifth century—are a number of 'Gothic' silver plate brooches from a series of sites in France (Troyes, valley of the Saône, Dept. of Aube) found in regions where the presence of the Alans is attested by historical evidence. Similar brooches of a somewhat more developed type were found in Spain, in one instance at Albacin near Granada, with parts of a gold necklace;

Fig. 69

a grave at Carthage in Tunisia had small characteristic Sarmatian gold plates.

ALANS IN THE TRAIN OF THE HUNS

The fifth century saw the end of the Hungarian Sarmatians. In 405 the Huns reached Hungary and by about AD 432 they were masters of most of the country, having subjugated the peoples living there, including the remaining Sarmatians.[6] A large contingent of Eastern Alans, the last Sarmatian group to enter Central Europe, must have arrived in the train of the Huns, as is indicated by contemporary Sarmatian graves in the Hungarian Plain containing pottery of the Hunnic type and incorporating other features of an eastern character. The grave from Hochfelden near Strasbourg may also be mentioned in this context. Its grave goods are of an international 'Gothic' character, but the mirror suggests that the person buried was a Sarmatian in the service of the Huns. After the death of Attila, the Hungarian Sarmatians freed themselves from Hunnic rule, only to be defeated in AD 472 by Theodoric, King of the Visigoths, when two Sarmatian Kings, Buka and Banai, fell in battle. Soon afterwards their country was seized by the Gepidae, and this seems to be the last reference in written records to the Hungarian Sarmatians, whom the Romans dubbed *Latrunculi* (free-booters, robbers)—even

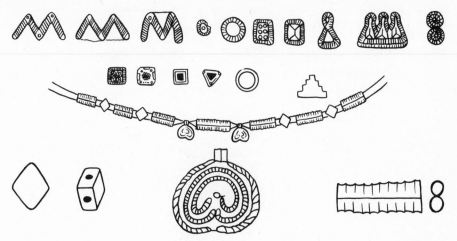

Fig. 69 Sarmatian ornaments and gold plaques (sewn on garments) from Austria, Spain and Africa (after Rostovtsev)

though they proved sufficiently formidable for six Roman emperors to take the title 'Sarmaticus' after defeating them, and special coins were several times minted to commemorate victories over them.

Plate 45

Some indication of the places settled by the Eastern Alans in Hunnic service is given by the names of modern Slavonic peoples.[7] The word 'Serb' for instance, is non-Slavonic. It is first mentioned by Pliny the Elder in the first century AD, and occurs in Ptolemy in the third century as the name of an Eastern Alan steppe-dwelling people somewhere north-east of the Sea of Azov, where, in the fourth century, they were presumably overrun by the Huns. At the beginning of the fifth century, Vibius Sequester says that 'the Elbe divides the Suevi from the Serbs'; and in the Middle Ages a country called 'White Serbia' embraced Saxony and Thuringia, i.e. an area within what was once the Hunnic Empire. Most likely, therefore, the detachment of the Hunnic army which controlled this region consisted chiefly of Eastern Alanic Serboi who, after the death of Attila, may have gained their independence. The indigenous Germans west of the

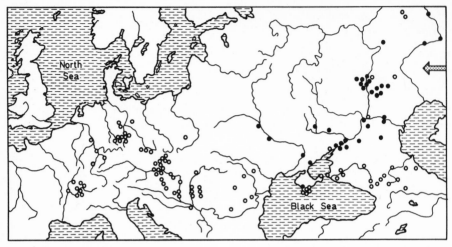

Fig. 70   Distribution of graves with deformed skulls in Europe. Dots represent skulls of the third and fourth centuries AD; circles represent skulls of the fifth and sixth centuries AD (after Werner, Klindt-Jensen and Sulimirski)

Fig. 70

Saale seem to have cast off the Alan yoke, but not the Slavs east of the river. It is interesting to note that the great concentration of artificially deformed skulls at the turn of the fifth century AD comes precisely from this region.

The most plausible conclusion is that the Alanic Serboi ultimately merged with the subjugated Slavonic population; the only trace of their sojourn there now is the Sorbs, a tiny group of Slavonic people in south-east Germany, also known by the name of Wends. Some such process presumably occurred in Yugoslav Serbia, where either another branch of the Alanic Serboi was concerned or, more probably, groups of Slavs led by already Slavicized Serboi arrived from the north.

Fig. 71

The word 'Croat' (Khorvat) has a similar history. The form 'Choroatos' and 'Chorouatos' has been found among inscrip-tions in ancient Tanais on the Don. According to the Byzantine Emperor Constantine Porphyrogenitus (AD 912–925), the 'Belochrobati' (White Croats), a Slav people, occupied the upper

Vistula and northern Bohemia. They exhibited certain Sarmatian characteristics noted by Arab travellers in the midtenth
century: besides the king, they had a viceroy called 'zhupan', a
nonSlavic term; the king was fed on mare's milk and the people
practised cranial deformation; the names of their chiefs were non
Slavonic. Opinion is divided as to whether the tribal name has a
Slavonic or Iranian etymology, but the arguments in favour of the
name, and consequently the people who first bore it, being of
Iranian origin are more convincing.

Here again we may conjecture that an East Alan tribe bearing
the name 'Choroatoi' or one similar to 'Croat' was entrusted
by the Huns with control of the region north of the Carpathians

*Fig. 71   Distribution in central and eastern Europe of topographic names connected with the
Sarmatians/Alans in Hunnic service in the fifth century AD, and of their richly furnished princely
burials. Dots: placenames of Alanic origin of the type Chotin, Chocen, Khoten, etc., derived
from the Sarmatian term denoting a fortified site or settlement; squares: placenames of Klwaty,
Harwaty, Charvátce type, connected with the settlement of Croats (after Łowmiański); crosses:
princely graves of Hunnic governors of the early fifth century AD in central Europe and parts of
eastern Europe*

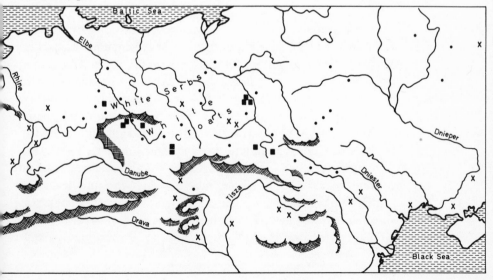

and Sudeten Mountains. The following is a list of place names of Alanic origin: Chotynec near Vytebet; Choten near Głusz-kowo; Chotimsk near Homel; Chocin on the Horyn near Równe; Chotyn on the Sluch; Chotyn near Dubno; Choten near Ostróg; Hotin on the Dniester; Choczen near Mozyr; Chotynicze near Pinsk; Chocin near Kałusz; Chocimierz near Tłumacz; Choceń near Włocławek; Choczeń near Sierpc; Chotum near Ciechanów; Chotyniec near Radymno; Chotynia near Garwolin; Chocim near Turek; Chotynin near Wieluń; Chocimów near Opatów; Chociny near Limanowa; Chocim (Kotzem) near Prudnik; Chotín near Hurbanovo; Chotiněves; Chotiň near Hradec Kralovy; Chotoun near Česki Brod; Chotěn-Köppelsdorf near Sonnenberg; Chotiniz-Köthenitz near Altenburg; Kötten near Tergau; Köthen near Bernburg; Kötschen near Merseburg; Kothen near Fulda; Kotzen near Brandenburg. After the eclipse of the Huns they may have ruled the country themselves, since there was no organized power capable of ousting them. They were ultimately Slavicized, and their name taken by the subject population, who were known as 'White (i.e. Western) Khorvats' or 'Croats', as the Serboi in Saxony were known as the 'White Serbs'.

The presence of Western Alans governing southern Poland on behalf of the Huns seems to be attested by some early-fifth-century princely graves. One, belonging to a Hunnic governor buried with his horse and a golden bow, his insignia of office, was found at Jakuszowice near Cracow. Another is the richly furnished burial at Jędrzychowice (Höckricht) near Wrocław. Among its grave goods was a cast-bronze kettle and a golden diadem set with almandines, both Hunnic, and a head ornament such as Alanic women wore. Other burials listed from east to west are: Bolshoy Kamenets near Kursk; Novogrigorievka on the Konka; Melitopol; Liman Tiligul; Concesti, Bessarabia; Buhăeni, Moldavia; Mojgrad in Transylvania; Apahida near Cluj; Szegednagyszéksos on the Tisa; Pecsüszög; Csorna;

Fig. 72

Plates 54–56

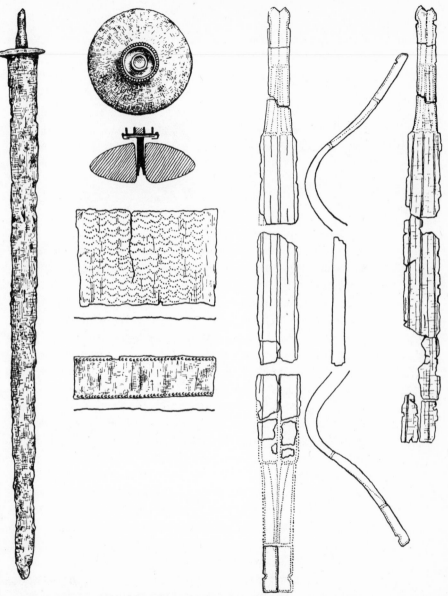

Fig. 72   Sword and a golden bow (an insignia of rank) from the burial of a Hunnic governor at Jakuszowice (after Inventaria Archaeologica, Poland)

Straže in Slovakia; Przemęczany north of Cracow; Wolfsheim near Wiesbaden; Altlussheim near Mainz; Flonheim near Worms; Mundolsheim near Strasbourg. The presence of Sar‚matians in Poland is further indicated by the names of ancient strongholds of the 'Hotin' type, and also by several place‚names connected with Croats. There are also several place‚names in Poland considered as derivative from the tribal name of the Serbs.[8]

ALANIC SURVIVALS IN EASTERN EUROPE

After the Hunnic disaster most of the Alanic tribes retreated westwards, but many remained in the steppe to be absorbed subsequently by the Huns and other Turkic peoples (Utiguri, Kutriguri, Khazars, Bolgars) who successively ruled over parts of the south of Eastern Europe. Some of the larger groups of Alans in the steppe managed to survive at least to the thirteenth century, when William of Rubruck encountered them between the Crimea and the Urals during his journey to Caracorum in Mongolia.

In the Ukraine we find a number of fourth‚ and fifth‚century Sarmatian graves on the lower Dnieper. Some scholars believe that they were left by Alans with a Hunnic strain. Characteristic of this group are the so‚called 'river graves', flat graves situated on the lowest river terraces submerged by the spring tides. In them warriors were buried, sometimes together with their horses, and they were rich in gold ornaments, weapons and decorated horse‚harness. Similar 'river‚graves' have also been discovered on the Volga and in some regions of Kazakhstan.

Probably also of Alanic origin are about a dozen richly furnished 'princely' graves, and graves of women wearing gold crowns set with semi‚precious stones or coloured glass; these are scattered over an enormous area from north Kazakhstan (Borovoe) to Hungary (Scorna) and Poland (Jędrzychowice, Jakuszowice). The most splendid example of such a crown was found in the grave of a woman at Kerch-Panticapaeum in the Crimea. It was an age-old custom in Eastern Europe, well represented in the remains of the second millennium BC, for women to wear elaborate diadems or decorative bands, and the custom was widespread among the Sarmatians/Alans (e.g. the splendid

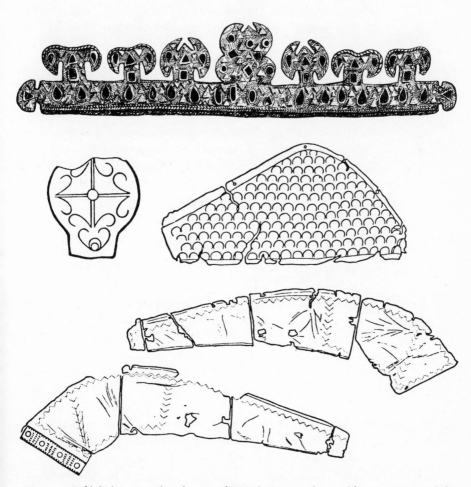

Fig. 73   Gold diadem set with amber, carnelian and garnet; a decorated bronze mirror, and thin gold foil which formed the decoration of a wooden saddle, all found in a princely burial at Melitopol in the Ukraine together with an iron sword with gold plated grip, several gold ornaments and a horse skeleton (after Peshanov)

Fig. 73

'crown' from Khokhlach-Novocherkassk). Burials with richly decorated 'Alanic' diadems of the Hunnic period are found in Eastern Europe exclusively within the area of Alanic settlement; two of them (Buhaeni, Conteşti), were in the region on the river Pruth ruled by the Alans (Antae).[9] The accompanying objects, an Alanic bronze mirror (Melitopol) or an Alanic kettle (Borovoe), attest the Alanic character of the burials. The custom was later adopted by the Huns, although Hunnic diadems (Kara-Agach) were of a different type.[10]

Another late Alanic people were the Antae, whom Jordanes considers to have been Slavonic (see Chapter V), adding that 'the Venedi (the Slavs), although of one stock, took on three names, i.e. Venedi, Antae and Sclavines'. However, this does not invalidate the identification of the Antae with the Alans/Asi: the Sarmatians evidently formed the area's ruling class, which was gradually Slavicized.[11] The process was probably completed not earlier than the sixth century, although many Sarmatian traditions remained. Among these are tamgas and beliefs associated with them, which spread to the conquered Slavonic population. The coats of arms of the Old Russian (Rus) Rurikovich dynasty, the central seat of which was Kiev, are derived from tamgas.

According to historical records, the rule of the Antae once subject to the Ostrogoths extended in the sixth century from the Dniester to the Dnieper and beyond. The centre of their kingdom must then have shifted eastwards to the Dnieper, where a large concentration of remains ascribed to them appears in the Kanev district.[12] The kingdom seems to have been overthrown by the Avars at the beginning of the seventh century. Several hoards of

Plate 59

valuable silverware, the property of the Antae, were buried at that time in the region of Kanev evidently in an attempt to preserve them from the conquering Avars. This coincides with the last mention of the name 'Antae' in historical records.

Small Alanic communities on the Black Sea coast, somewhere near Kherson, are noted in the thirteenth century. Other small groups of Alans, who sought refuge in the Crimea and partly merged with the Goths, are mentioned as late as the seventeenth century, when they were still practising cranial deformation. They probably lived mainly on the southern coast. In about 1240, Theodorus was Bishop of the Alans, and in the fourteenth century the region between Feodosia (Theodosia) and Alusha bore the name 'Alania', and was claimed by both the Archbishop of Kherson and Archbishop of Gotia as part of their arch-dioceses, the Alans having been introduced to Christianity in the tenth century.

Archaeological remains of the fifth to the seventh century, attributable—at least partly—to the Alans, have been found in southern Crimea in the region south-east of Sevastopol, and on the south-eastern coast, in Taurion, including the famous cemetery of Suuk-Su which consists mainly of Gothic burials;[13] many of the graves exhibit features characteristic of the Alans, including cranial deformation.

Mention may also be made of the group of Alans who finished up furthest from their homeland. Orthodox Christian Asu (Alans), evidently of East European origin, formed part of the Mongol army in China; strangest of all, 30,000 Orthodox Christian Alans are mentioned in 1318 by Brother Pellegrini, Bishop of Zaytun in China, as living with their families on the Chinese coast opposite Formosa. They are said to have been 'in the Great King's pay', but nothing more is known about them. They were probably forcibly transferred to China in the twelfth or, more likely, in the thirteenth century.

THE ALANS IN THE CAUCASUS

Finally, we come to the Alans of the Caucasus.[14] Their modern descendants, the Ossetinians, a tiny race living in the Caucasian highland, are the only people still to speak—although in a considerably corrupted form—the language of the once numerous and mighty Sarmatians.

Sarmatian tribes reaching the Caucasus in the fourth century BC and later kept exclusively to the foothills and the adjoining steppe. After the Hunnic invasion the large groups of Alans from the lower Volga steppes who again entered the region partly settled in the foothills, merging with their fellow Sarmatians who had arrived before them, but for the most part deeply penetrated the mountain area. Their main body entered the central Caucasian highland, populating the whole area which had formerly been characterized by the Iron Age Koban culture.

The Caucasian Alans survived the Avar onslaught at the end of the sixth century, then that of the Altai Turks; from about AD 650 they were under the suzerainty of the Khazars, being mentioned often in contemporary annals. We hear, for instance, that in AD 558, Justinian, son of Germanus, the Roman commander in Colchis, received a message from Sarus (or Sarozi), King of the Alans, to the effect that Candrich, King of the Avars, wished to open relations with the Emperor. The name of another Alan ruler, Itaz, is mentioned in the eighth century. The whole country east of the Kuban valley up to Dagestan was named 'Alania'. This area was ruled over by the Alans whose princes and princesses often intermarried with the royal house of Georgia in Transcaucasia. When the Alans entered this country in the fourth century AD, they subdued the local tribes who were of a different stock, and lived side by side with the natives in the same villages, although they buried their dead in different cemeteries. This relationship affected both cultures, but ultimately the Alans were absorbed by the aboriginal inhabitants who probably outnumbered them.

Alanic graves are also found in Dagestan, but in its later stages the specifically Alan culture shrank considerably. The first to disappear were its eastern and western extremities until finally the area was confined solely to the northern foothills of the central region, due to a gradual cultural absorption of the Alans by the indigenous population. But the country was still known as Alania, and the Alans are frequently mentioned in written records.

It was the Tartar-Mongol invasion in the twelfth and thirteenth centuries which ended the Alans' existence; their name is never referred to again and 'Alania' disappears from written sources. In their place we now encounter the names of the modern north Caucasian peoples, whose culture was evidently derived from that of the Alans.

Typical of the culture of the true medieval north Caucasian Alans are 'catacomb' graves strewn with charcoal, continuing the tradition which they brought with them from the lower Volga steppes. Cranial deformation is found only in the earliest graves, and the custom was entirely abandoned by the eighth century AD. Generally speaking, the graves are poorly furnished, clay vessels being the usual grave goods. Their pottery underwent certain changes, marking three main stages in the development of the culture; the stages cover the fifth to the seventh, the eighth to the ninth, and the tenth to the eleventh century respectively. Other grave goods are rare, but include such ornaments as bronze brooches, silver ear-pendants, bronze mirrors and small bronze or silver plates sewn on to garments. In a few cases an iron sword and iron bits were excavated and also sixth-century Byzantine coins and gold bracelets of the ninth century. Richly furnished graves are found only in cemeteries of the last period.

The graves of the final period differ in many respects from the earlier ones, the most typical being those in the cemetery at Zmeyskaya. The majority were equipped with weapons and many with horse harness. The usual weapons are sabres of the so-called Khazar type, common in East Europe during the whole Early Medieval period, their wooden sheaths often covered with thin, richly ornamented gold, silver or bronze foil. Bows are common, but only a few spear-heads were found. Foot warriors had iron double-edged battle-axes; William of Rubruck (thirteenth century) says that 'the Alans are good makers of weapons',

Fig. 74

Plate 60

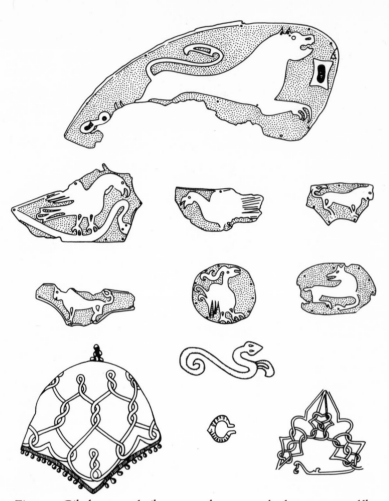

Fig. 74 Gilt bronze and silver personal ornament, head ornaments, saddle decorations, etc., from Alanic catacomb graves at Zhmeyskaya in the north-east Caucasus, tenth-twelfth centuries AD (after Kuznetsov)

implying that they had a wide appreciation of them. Up to four fully developed, profusely decorated cavalry saddles are found in a single grave. The decoration sometimes includes gold plates, and the horse harness is similarly embellished. The figural ornament on these objects is connected with the Early Iron Age Koban style of the central Caucasian highland, and must have been derived from it. No helmets, shields or mail-armour were found.

Bronze or glass bracelets, beads mainly made of glass or amber, and other personal ornaments are the usual equipment of female burials. The abundance of amber is striking and points to connections with the Kiev region and the Baltic amber coast. Social differentiation is reflected in the equipment.

Relations were maintained with Georgia and Armenia, the Arabic east, Byzantium and Kievan Russia. However, the western and eastern areas of Alanic territory differed in this respect, as can be seen from the style and type of Christian churches which still exist, although the country is now over-whelmingly Moslem. Those in the western area were Byzantine, due to the presence of Byzantine missionaries, while those in the central highland, the area of the Georgian missions, were of the Georgian type. The different names, 'Alania' and 'As', given to the two parts of the country by medieval writers suggest a political division of the territory.

Lastly the Saltovo-Maiaki culture should be mentioned,[15] as it is considered to have been Alanic by several scholars. It is represented by a large number of graves and settlements found in two main regions rather far from one another, with only very few sites in between. One region lies in the valley of the lower Don and its few western tributaries; the other covers a large area in the upper Donetz basin in the Ukrainian forest-steppe zone. The people of the culture were settled farmers and cattle-breeders, and at the same time, skilled artisans. Two somewhat diverse types of settlement and grave have been distinguished, probably left by different groups of people, one of them possibly the Alans. The culture lasted for about 200–250 years, from the eighth to the tenth century AD.

The strong similarities between several objects of the Saltovo-Maiaki culture and the north Caucasian Alanic culture of the

Fig. 75

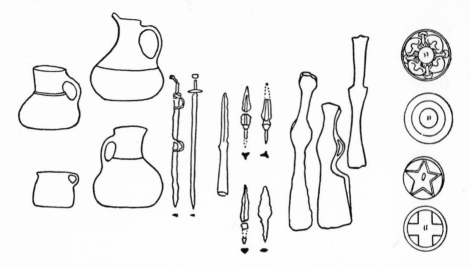

early stage (fourth century AD) have led some scholars to regard the Saltovo-Maiaki people as Alanic colonists who migrated from the Caucasus; but this is invalidated by the distance separating the two groups of the Saltovo-Maiaki culture from the Caucasus (some 400 miles in one case, more than 600 miles in the other) and by the time lag of 400 years dividing the Caucasian remains, typical of the Late Sarmatian period, from those of the Saltovo-Maiaki culture.

CONCLUSION

There is an element of sadness in the fate of the Sarmatians, whose chequered history we have briefly reviewed. At different points in time their peoples and tribes were driven into almost every western European country, and they were forced eastwards as far as China. The descendants of those who came to England in AD 175 probably still live somewhere in the country. Sarmatian history is difficult to disentangle from that of many peoples and nations, and for many centuries the whole eastern

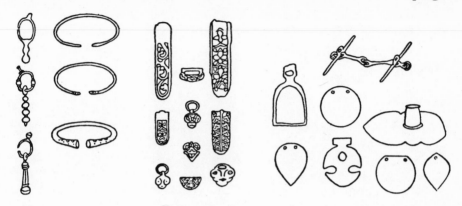

Fig. 75   Finds characteristic of the Saltovo-Maiaki culture of the eighth-ninth centuries AD (after Merpert)

part of Europe was called 'Sarmatia' after them. They are now almost forgotten. Little remains to remind the modern world of their existence—the Ossetinians, the names of a few Slavonic peoples and words of Sarmatian (Iranian) origin in Slavonic languages, some European place-names, items in Polish heraldry (abolished in 1920), a vague tradition of Sarmatian origin lingering among sections of the Polish nobility, and an increasing number of objects recovered by archaeologists. That is all. The part they played in the formation of the various Slavonic nations has been all but obliterated by later expansions of eastern nomads —the Avars, Bulgars, and Magyars, who did not reach Western Europe.

The Sarmatians were a 'barbaric' people; but they contributed to the development of the splendid Sarmato-Bosporan art, and to its 'Gothic' successor, which later generated many branches of medieval Western European art—Merovingian, Anglo-Saxon, Romanesque. But here again their influence has usually been passed over in silence.

Notes on the Text

Abbreviations

AA	*Artibus Asiae,* Ascona
AAASH	*Acta Archaeologica Academiae Scientiarum Hungaricae,* Budapest
AH	*Archaeologia Hungarica,* Budapest
AK	*Arkheologiya, Kiev* (in Ukrainian)
AO	*Arkheologicheskie Otkritiya,* Moscow 1966 and 1967
AP	*Arkheologichni Pamyatky USSR,* Kiev (in Ukrainian)
ASE	*Arkheologicheskii Sbornik, Hermitage,* Leningrad
Bulletin	*Bulletin of the University of London Institute of Archaeology*
ESA	*Eurasia Septentrionalis Antiqua,* Helsinki
IANK	*Izvestiya Akademii Nauk Kazakhstanskoy SSR,* Alma Ata
IGAIMK	*Izvestiya Gos. Akademii Istorii Materialnoy Kultury,* Leningrad
KDSZK	*Kultura Drevnikh Skotovodov i Zemledeltsev Kazakhstana,* Alma Alta 1969
KSIAK	*Kratkie Soobshcheniya Instituta Arkheologii, Kiev*
KSIAM	*Kratkie Soobshcheniya Instituta Archeologii AN SSSR, Moscow*
KSIE	*Kratkie Soobshcheniya Instituta Etnografii,* Moscow
KSIIMK	*Kratkie Soobshcheniya Instituta Materialnoy Kultury,* Moscow and Leningrad
MCA	*Materiale și cercetari arheologice,* Bucharest (in Romanian)
MDAPV	*Materialy i Doslizhdeniya z Arkheologii Prykapattya i Volyni,* Kiev (in Ukrainian)
MIA	*Materialy i Issledovaniya po Arkheologii SSSR,* Moscow and Leningrad
PR	*The Polish Review,* New York
Rapports	*Les Rapports et les Informations des Archéologues de l'URSS VI Congrès Internat. des Sciences Préhist. et Protohistoriques,* Moscow 1962
SA	*Sovetskaya Arkheologiya,* Moscow
Sb.Art.	*Issledovaniya po Arkheologii SSSR (Artamonov Festschrift),* Leningrad 1961

SCIV   *Studii şi cercetări di Istorie Veche,* Bucharest (in Romanian)
SE   *Sovetskaya Etnografiya,* Moscow
SVOD   *Svod Arkheologicheskikh Istochnikov. Arkheologiya SSSR,* Moscow and Leningrad
TIIAEK   *Trudy Instituta Istorii, Arkheologii i Etnografii Akademii Nauk Kazakhstanskoy SSR,* Alma Ata
VDI   *Vyestnik Drevney Istorii,* Moscow
VSSA   *Voprosy Skifo-Sarmatskoy Arkheologii,* Moscow 1954

CHAPTER I

1   E. V. Chernenko, Skifskii boyovi poyasy, *AK* XVI, 1964, pp. 24–44; Shkiryani pantsyri skifskoho chasu, *AK* XVII, 1964, pp. 144–52; Pantsyri skifskoho chasu, *AK* XVIII, 1965, pp. 77–104.

2   S. P. Tolstov, 1948, pp. 224–7; 1962, pp. 149–50, fig. 82. B. Rubin, *Die Entstehung der Kataphraktenreiterei im Lichte der chorezmischen Aus-grabungen. Historia,* IV, Wiesbaden 1955, pp. 264–83.

3   A. M. Tallgren, Portable Altars, *ESA* XI, 1937, pp. 47–68.

CHAPTER II

1   The works by K. F. Smirnov of 1961, 1964 and 1963 (jointly with V. G. Petrenko); his articles in: *SA* 1957, 3, pp. 3 ff., and 1964, 3, pp. 45 ff.; *KSIIMK* 34, 1950, pp. 97 ff.; *VSSA,* pp. 195–219. Also I. V. Sinitsyn, *KSIIMK* 32, 1950, pp. 101 ff.; *TIIAEK* 1, 1956, pp. 87–139; and V. P. Shilov, *AO* 1966, pp. 87–88.

2   I. P. Berkhin-Zasetskaya and L. Ia. Malovitskaya, *SA* 1965, 3, pp. 143–53; E. K. Maksimov, *SA* 1966, I, pp. 51–60.

3   A. A. Yessen, *SA* XVIII, 1953, pp. 49–110; *VSSA,* pp. 112–31. A. I. Terenozhkin, 1961, pp. 102 ff. A. A. Shchepinskii, *KSIAK* 12, 1962, pp. 57 ff. G. T. Kovpanenko, *KSIAK* 12, 1962, pp. 66 ff. A. N. Melentiev, *KSIAM* 112, 1967, pp. 38 ff. E. K. Maksimov, *SA* 1963, 3, pp. 282 ff.

4   J. D. P. Bolton, 1962. Herodotus, *Histories,* Rawlinson's translation revised and annotated by A. W. Lawrence, Oxford 1935.

5   M. Vasmer, *Untersuchungen über die ältesten Wohnsitze der Slaven :* I *Die Iranier in Südrussland,* Leipzig 1923, p. 14.

6 S. P. Tolstov, the works of 1948 and 1962, and his articles in: *SE* 1961, 4, pp. 114–46; *VDI* 1963, 2, pp. 23–45; and jointly with M. A. Itina in: *SA* 1966, 2, pp. 151–75 and 1968, 2, pp. 151 ff.

7 S. I. Rudenko, *SVOD*. M. I. Artamonov, 1966. K. Jettmar, 1967. N. Fettich, *AAASH* II, 1952, pp. 251–267.

8 M. N. Komarova, *ASE* 5, 1962, pp. 50–75.

9 M. P. Griaznov, *KSIIKM* 61, 1956, pp. 8 ff. K. Akishev, *TIIAEK* 7, 1957, pp. 4–31. E. I. Ageeva and A. G. Maksimova, *TIIAEK* 7, 1957, pp. 32–57. S. S. Chernikov, *KSIIMK* 53, 1954, pp. 29–49. G. B. Zdanovich, *KDSZK*, pp. 68 ff.

10 M. K. Kardybaev, *TIIAEK* 7, 1957, pp. 162–97; *IANK* 1, 6, 1958, pp. 95–108, and 1, 18, 1962, pp. 70–83; *Novoe v Arkheologii Kazakhstana,* Alma Ata 1968, pp. 21–36. See also: P. S. Rykov, *IGAIMK* 110, 1935, p. 49; M. P. Griaznov, *SA* XVI, 1952, pp. 129 ff.; A. M. Orazbaev, *KDSZK*, pp. 175 ff.

11 M. P. Griaznov, *IGAIMK* 110, 1935, pp. 192 ff. S. S. Chernikov, *MIA* 88, 1960. S. V. Zolotova, *KSIAM* 101, 1964, pp. 61 ff.

12 V. N. Poltoratskaya, *ASE* 3, 1961, pp. 74–88.

13 M. P. Griaznov, *KSIIMK* 18, 1947, pp. 9–17. M. P. Zavitukhina, *ASE* 3, 1961, pp. 89–108.

14 A. N. Bernshtam, *SA* XL, 1949, pp. 337–59. S. S. Chernikov, *KSIIMK* 73, 1959, pp. 103 ff.; *KSIAM* 98, 1964, pp. 29–32. A. G. Maksimova, *KSIIMK* 80, 1960, pp. 60 ff.; *KDSZK*, pp. 136 ff. V. V. Ginsburg, *KSIE* XIX, 1952, pp. 84 ff. K. A. Akishev and G. A. Kushaev, 1963.

15 E. G. Pulleyblank, Chinese and Indo-Europeans, *Journal of the Royal Asiatic Society,* 1966, pp. 9–39.

16 S. I. Rudenko, 1960. A. D. Grach, *SA* 1967, 3, pp. 215–33. Ia. I. Sunchugashev, *SA* 1964, 3, pp. 301 ff., and 1966, 4, pp. 187 ff.

17 N. L. Tchlenova, *Rapports* VII, pp. 191–200; *Rapports* VI; *Artibus Asiae* XXVI, 1963, pp. 27–70; *MIA* 115, 1962, pp. 167–203.

18 N. L. Tchlenova, 1967.

CHAPTER III

1 E. I. Ageeva and A. G. Maksimova, *TIIAEK* 7, 1959, pp. 32–44. F. Ch. Arslanova, *IANK* 2, 19, 1962, pp. 76–93.

2 M. G. Moshkova, *SVOD* 1963. K. F. Smirnov, *VSSA*, pp. 200 ff.;

KSIAM 89, 1962, pp. 83–93 and 107, 1966, pp. 33–43. M. Ch. Sadykova, *MIA* 115, 1962, pp. 242 ff.

3 K. F. Smirnov, *VDI* 1948, 1, pp. 213–19; *KSIIMK* 34, 1950, pp. 97–113.

4 Ch. M. Danoff, Pontos Euxeinos. *Real-Encyklopädie, Pauly-Wissowa,* IX, 1962, pp. 866–1175.

5 A. L. Mongait, *Archaeology in the USSR* (translated by M. W. Thompson), Harmondsworth 1961, pp. 202 ff. V. P. Shilov, *SA* 1961, 1, pp. 150–68. I. B. Brashinskii and Ia. V. Domanskii, *AO* 1966, pp. 80–3.

6 T. N. Knipovich, 1949. D. B. Shelov, *MIA* 98, 1961; *AO* 1965, pp. 120–3. A. I. Boltunova, *AO* 1966, pp. 83–5.

7 K. F. Smirnov, *MIA* 64, 1958, pp. 272 ff., 310–12. N. V. Anfimov, *SA* XI, 1949, pp. 241–60; *MIA* 23, 1951, pp. 155 ff.

8 D. T. Berezovets, *AP* X, 1961, p. 59, fig. 4.

9 A. Bydłowski, *Światowit* V, 1904, p. 59. V. A. Illinska; *AP* VII, 1957. M. I. Vyazmitina, *AP* VII, 1953 and VIII, 1960, pp. 63 ff. B. N. Grakov, *Skify,* Kiev 1947; *MIA* 115, 1962, pp. 86 ff.; *KSIIMK* 34, 1950, pp. 10 ff. B. V. Firshteyn, *Voprosy Antropologii* 22, 1966, p. 56. D. T. Berezovets, *AP* IX, 1960, pp. 39–87.

10 D. M. Pippidi and D. Berciu, *Din Istoria Dobrogei* I, Bucharest 1965, pp. 113 ff. M. Rostovtzeff, 1922, pp. 80 ff.

11 P. D. Liberov, *VSSA,* pp. 143 ff.; *MIA* 151, 1969. M. I. Vyazmitina, *VSSA,* pp. 220–44. D. Ia. Telegin, *KSIAK* 8, pp. 48 ff. E. F. Pokrovska, *AK* X, 1957, pp. 65 ff. and XI, 1957, pp. 148–53. D. T. Berezovets, *AP* IX, 1960, pp. 39–87. M. P. Abramova, *MIA* 115, 1962, pp. 280 ff. M. S. Sinitsyn, *Materialy po Arkheologii Severnogo Prichernomorya* 4, Odessa 1962, pp. 56 f. B. N. Grakov, *ASE* 6, 1964, pp. 118–27.

12 A. I. Terenozhkin, *KSIAK* 5, 1955, pp. 23–34. E. F. Pokrovskaya, *VDI* 1955, 2, pp. 191–9.

13 D. Ia. Telegin, the article quoted in note 11; for similar pottery see K. F. Smirnov, 1964, figs 45:5b and 67:14.

14 B. N. Grakov, *Kamenskoe Gorodishche na Dnepre, MIA* 36, 1954, pp. 155 ff. N. N. Pogrebova, *MIA* 64, 1958, pp. 108–271.

15 B. A. Shramko, *KSIAM* 91, 1962, pp. 72–77; *SA* 1969, 3, pp. 53–70.

CHAPTER IV

1   E. G. Pulleyblank, Chinese and Indo-Europeans, *Journal of the Royal Asiatic Society*, 1966, p. 35.

2   E. I. Ageeva, *TIIAEK* 12, 1961, pp. 21–40; *IANK* 3, 11, 1959, pp. 80–5. K. A. Akishev and G. A. Kushaev, 1963, pp. 137 ff. A. K. Abetekov and Iu. D. Baruzdin, 1963, pp. 17–31. A. N. Bernshtam, *MIA* 26, 1952; in *Po Sledam Drevnikh Kultur,* Moscow 1954, pp. 261–304. N. G. Gorbunova, *ASE* 3 1961, pp. 171–94; *SA*, 1962, 4, pp. 37–48. S. S. Chernikov, *KSIIMK* 73, 1959, pp. 103 ff. V. V. Ginsburg, *KSIE* XIV, 1952, pp. 84–90. O. Ismagulov, *TIIAEK* 16, 1962, pp. 168–91. M. P. Griaznov, *MIA* 48, 1956, pp. 44 ff. M. P. Zavitukhina, *ASE* 3, 1961, pp. 89–108. V. N. Pol-toratskaya, *ASE* 3, 1961, p. 85.

3   A. M. Khazanov, in *Materialnaya Kultura Narodov Sredney Azii i Kazakhstana,* Moscow 1966, pp. 29–44. B. A. Litvinskii, *SA* 1966, 4, pp. 51–69. A. F. Medvedev, *KSIAM* 102, 1964, pp. 3–7. G. Rausing, The Bow. Some Notes on its Origin and Development. Lund 1967, *Acta Archaeologica Lundensia*, No. 6.

4   M. K. Kardyrbaev, *TIIAEK* 7, 1957, p. 193.

5   B. N. Grakov, *VDI* 1947, 3, pp. 105 ff. K. F. Smirnov, *KSIIMK* 34, 1950, pp. 102 ff.

6   M. P. Abramova, *SA* 1959, 1, pp. 52–71; 1969, 2, pp. 69–84. I. V. Sinitsyn, *KSIIMK* 32, 1950, pp. 101 ff. K. F. Smirnov, *KSIIMK* 34, 1950, pp. 97 ff.; *VSSA*, pp. 195 ff. E. K. Maksimov, *SA* 1957, 4, pp. 157 ff. M. Kh. Salnikova, *MIA* 115, 1962, pp. 242–73. V. P. Shilov, *KSIIMK* 59, 1955, pp. 118–128.

7   N. V. Anfimov, *MIA* 23, 1951, pp. 144 ff., 169 ff. P. M. Muchaev, *SA* 1965, 2, pp. 174 ff. V. B. Vinogradov, *SA* 1968, 1, pp. 48–55. K. M. Skalon, *Trudy Otdela Istorii Pervobytnoy Kultury* I, Leningrad 1941; M. P. Abramova, *SA* 1966, 1, pp. 51–60.

8   M. Smiszko, *Wiadomości Archeologiczne* XIII, Warsaw 1935, pp. 155–9. L. I. Krushelnitskaya, *KSIAM* 105, 1965, pp. 119–20; *MDAPV* 5, 1964, pp. 135 ff. Iu. V. Kukharenko, *SA* 1959, 1, pp. 31–54. V. I. Bidzila, *AK* XVII, 1964, pp. 92–143. D. Popescu, *Istoria Rominei* I, Bucharest 1960, pp. 232 ff. D. Berciu, *Bulletin* 6, 1967, pp. 75–93. A. I. Meliukova, *MIA* 64, 1958, pp. 90 ff.; SA 1962, 1, pp. 195 ff. L. Iakounina-Ivanova, *ESA* I, 1927, pp. 100–9. A. K.

Ambroz, *SVOD*, A⁄1⁄30, 1966, pl. 18, maps 1, 2. I. I. Gushchina, *SA* 1961, 2, pp. 241–6. A. A. Bodianskii, *SA* 1962, 1, pp. 272 ff. D. A. Mochinskii, *Arkheologia Starogo i Novogo Sveta,* Moscow 1962, pp. 82–96. R. Vulpe, *Le Problème des Bastarnes à la Lumière des Découvertes Archéologiques en Moldavie,* Bucharest 1955. V. P. Petrov, in *Materialy po Arkheologii Severnogo Prichernomorya* IV, Odessa 1962, pp. 227–234.

9 M. I. Vyazmitina, 1962, pp. 230 ff.; *MIA* 150, 1969, pp. 119–34. N. N. Pogrebova, *KSIAK* 7, 1957, pp. 67 f. Reports by A. V. Dobro⁄ volskii and others in *AP* IX, 1960, pp. 141–209.

10 N. N. Pogrebova, *MIA* 96, 1961, pp. 103–213.

11 P. N. Shults, *KSIIMK* 21, 1947, pp. 16–21; Shults and V. P. Babenchikov, in *Istoriya i Arkeologiya Drevnego Kryma,* Kiev 1957, pp. 61–93, 94–141. O. D. Dashevskaya, *MIA* 64, 1958, pp. 248–71. N. N. Pogrebova, *KSIIMK* 21, 1941, pp. 22–32. For Scythian coins minted in Olbia, see A. G. Salnikov in *Zapiski Odesskogo Arkheolo⁄ gicheskogo Obshchestva* I, 34, Odessa 1960, pp. 85–95.

12 M. Iu. Smishko, *MDAPV* 4, 1962, pp. 54–70.

13 K. F. Smirnov, *VDI* 1948, 1, pp. 213 ff. M. I. Vyazmitina, *AK* VIII, 1953, pp. 56 ff; *VSSA*, pp. 220–44; in *Narysy Starodavnoy Istorii Ukrainskoy RSR,* pp. 218 ff. E. V. Makhno, *AP* IX, 1960, pp. 14–38. Reports by several authors in *AP* X, 1961.

14 A. I. Meliukova, *MIA* 115, 1962, pp. 114–66.

15 I. P. Zasetskaya, *ASE* 7, 1965, pp. 28–35. O. Klindt⁄Jensen, *Gundestrupkedelen,* 1961. D. F. Allen, *Numismatic Chronicle* Seventh Series, VIII, 1968, pp. 37–54.

CHAPTER V

1 K. V. Salnikov, *MIA* 1, 1940, pp. 121–38. K. F. Smirnov, *KSIIMK* 34, 1950, pp. 111 ff.; *SA* XVII, 1953, pp. 133 ff.; *VSSA*, pp. 203 ff.; *KSIAM* 107, 1966, pp. 33–43. Articles by the same author and by I. V. Sinitsin, and V. P. Shilov in *MIA* 60, 1959 and 78, 1960. I. P. Berkin, *ASE* 2, 1961, pp. 141 ff. M. G. Moshkova, *MIA* 115, pp. 222 ff. M. Kh. Sadykova, *MIA* 115, 1962, pp. 258. T. G. Oboldueva, *AP* IV, 1952, pp. 43–47.

2 A. I. Meliukova, *SA* 1962, 1, pp. 195 ff.

3 M. I. Rostovtsev, 1922 and 1929. E. H. Minns, The Art of the

Northern Nomads. *Proceedings of the British Academy* XXVIII, 1943, pp. 28 ff.

4 A. M. Apakidze and others, *Mtskheta* I, Tbilisi 1958, pp. 25–151, 208–33, and 276–86 (a summary in English).

5 S. P. Tolstov, *SE* VI–VII, 1947, pp. 39–57.

6 H. Humbach, in *Die Welt der Slaven* VI, Munich 1961, pp. 225 ff.

7 E. I. Solomonik, 1959; in *Istoriya i Arkheologiya Kryma,* Kiev 1957, pp. 210 ff. T. Sulimirski in *PR* IX, New York 1964, pp. 50 ff.

8 A few cemeteries described in *AP* XIII, 1963, by E. V. Veymarn, pp. 15–42, V. P. Babenchykov, pp. 90–123, and K. F. Sokolova, pp. 124–7.

9 N. P. Kondakov, I. I. Tolstoy and S. Reinach, 1891, pp. 489–96. M. I. Rostovtsev, 1922, 1931. M. A. Miller, 1958, pp. 95 ff. K. M. Skalon, *ASE* 2, 1961, pp. 114–40. S. I. Kaposhina, *Antiquity* XXXVII, 1963, pp. 256 ff.

10 M. I. Vyazmitina, *AK* VIII, 1953, pp. 60 ff. B. N. Grakov, *MIA* 115, 1962, pp. 56–113. Reports by several authors in *AP* X, 1961. E. V. Makhno, *AP* IX, 1960, pp. 14–38. For the burial from Traiany near Balta, mentioned above, see *Otchet Imper. Arkheol. Kommisii* for 1913–15, St Petersburg 1918, p. 201, fig. 255.

11 For the Chernyakhiv culture see E. V. Makhno, *MIA* 82, 1960; I. I. Liapushkin, *MIA* 104, 1961; also articles by several authors in *MIA* 116, 1964. For the cemetery of Kantemirivka see M. Ia. Rudynskii, *Zapysky Vseukrainskoho Arkheol. Komitetu* I, Kiev, 1931 and E. V. Makhno, *AP* III, 1952.

12 V. V. Kropotkin, 1961; 1967; *SVOD* 1-4-4, 1961; T. Sulimirski in *Archeologia Polski* XI, 1966, pp. 148 ff.

13 These topics have been discussed, and the relevant literature quoted, in my article 'Sarmatians in the Polish Past' cited in note 7.

14 The relevant literature quoted in my article note 12. Added may be: S. Morinz and Gh. Bichir, *MCA* VI, 1959, pp. 487–95. R. Vulpe, *Dacia*, New Series, V. 1961, pp. 365–93. B. Mitrea, *SCIV* 2-XIII, 1962, pp. 431–5. A. Andronic, *SCIV* 2–XIV, 1963, pp. 347–60. Gh. Diaconu, *SCIV* 2–XIV, 1963, pp. 323–45. I. Ioniţa, *Arheologia Moldovei* II–III, Iasi 1964, pp. 311–28.

15 The works by M. Parducz, 1941, 1944, 1950 and 1956; and by J. Harmatta, 1950.

16   I. A. Richmond and E. A. Thompson, *Journal of Roman Studies* XXXIV, 1944, and XLVI, 1956.

CHAPTER VI

1   Articles by several authors in *MIA* 70, 1959. E. V. Makhno, *SA* XXIII, 1955, pp. 81 ff.; *MIA* 82, 1960. P. N. Tretiakov, *SA* 1960, 1, pp. 36–46. Iu. V. Kukharenko, *SA* 1960, 1, pp. 289 ff.; M. A. Tikhanova, *SA* 1957, 4, pp. 168 ff. Articles by several authors in *MIA* 116, 1964, and in *Istoriya i Arkheologiya Yugo-Zapada SSSR*, Moscow 1967.

2   B. Mitrea, *Dacia*, New Series, III, 1959, pp. 473 ff. I. Ioniţa, *Arheologia Moldovei* IV, Iaşi 1966, pp. 188–259.

3   N. Åberg, 1922. N. Fettich, 1932. W. A. v. Jenny and W. F. Volbach, *Germanischer Schmuck des frühen Mittelalters*, Berlin 1933. I. Korvig, *AAASH* 10, 1959, pp. 209–25. A. K. Ambroz, *SVOD* 1966, map pl. 25:3. V. A. Kuznetsov and V. K. Pudovin, *SA* 1961, 2, pp. 78 ff. H. Zeiss, *Die Grabfunde aus dem spanischen West-gotenreich*, Berlin and Leipzig 1934, pp. 12 ff., 81 ff. J. Werner, *Katalog d. Sammlung Diergardt* I, Berlin 1961.

4   A. Longdon, *Géographie de la Gaule au VIe siècle*, Paris 1878, pp. 168 f.; *Les noms de lieu de la France*, Paris 1920, pp. 130. G. Jeanton, *Les invasions barbares et le peuplement de l'Europe*. Centre International de Synthèse et Institut International d'Archéocivilisation, Paris 1953. L. Franchet, Une colonie Scytho-Alaine en Orléanais au Ve siècle. *Revue Scientifique. Revue Rose,* 68 année, Paris 1930, pp. 70–82, 109–17.

5   E. Beninger, 1931. A. Alföldi, 1932. J. Werner, 1956. The Alano-Sarmatian character of most of the finds published has not been specified.

6   M. Parducz, 1963. D. J. Csallány, 1961. E. A. Thompson, 1948. The Alsatian graves from Hochfelden and Mundolsheim (see J. J. Hatt, *Gallia* XXIII, 1965, pp. 250–6; J. Werner, 1956, p. 52, pl. 62) seem to have been of Alans of higher rank in the Hunnic service.

7   These topics have been discussed, and the relevant literature quoted, in my article *PR* IX, 1964. See also T. Lewicki, *Liber Iosephi Kos-trzewski Octogenario*, Wrocław, Warsaw and Cracow, 1968, pp. 363–76.

8   G. László, The Significance of the Hun Golden Bow, *AAASH* I,

1951. E. Kucharski, Żywioł alański (jaski) w Karpatach Wschodnich. *Papers read at the Conference on Polish Carpathians in Cracow,* Warsaw 1938. T. Lewicki, *Roczniki Historyczne* XXVII, 1956, map on p. 31, reproduced by the author in *PR* IX, p. 48; *Materiały Archeologiczne* VIII, Cracow 1967, pp. 25–31. H.Łowmiański, vol. II, 1964, map on p. 199. See also the article by K. Jażdżewski on the Germano-Slavonic relations since the Hunnic invasion of Central Europe, in *Prace i Materiały Muzeum Arch. i Etnograf.,* No. 5, Łódź 1960, pp. 51–77.

9 N. Fettich, *AH* XXXII, 1953. A. Florescu, *Dacia* IV, 1960, pp. 261 ff. I. F. Kovaleva, *SA* 1962, pp. 233–8. I. S. Kamenetskii and V. V. Kropotkin, *SA* 1962, 3, pp. 235 ff. I. Ioniţa, *Arheologia Modovei* II/III, 1964, pp. 311–28.

10 J. Werner, 1956, pl. 31. K. Skalon, *ASE* 2, 1961, pp. 120 ff. V. F. Peshanov, *KSIAK* 11, 1961, pp. 70–4.

11 G. Vernadsky, Goten und Anten in Südrussland, *Süddeutsche Forschungen* III, Munich 1938; On the Origin of the Antae, *Journal of the American Oriental Society* 59, New Haven 1939, pp. 56 ff. N. Zupanić, L'origine et le nom des Antes, *Etnolog* VII, Ljubljana 1934, pp. 88 ff., 97 ff.

12 P. M. Tretiakov, *SE* 1947, 4, pp. 71–83. B. A. Rybakov, *SA* XVII, 1953, pp. 23–104.

13 N. P. Repnikov, *Izvestia Imp. Arch. Kom.* 19, 1906. V. V. Kropotkin, *SA* 1959, 1, pp. 181 ff.

14 *Arkheologicheskie Raskopki v Rayone Zmeyskoy Severnoy Osetii,* Ordzhonikidze 1961; articles by S. S. Kussaeva, pp. 51–61, and V. A. Kuznetsov, pp. 62–135. L. G. Nechaeva, *Sb.Art.,* pp. 151–9. Iu. S. Gagloyti, 1966.

15 N. Ia. Merpert, *KSIIMK* 36, 1951, pp. 14–30. I. I. Ljapushkin, *MIA* 62, 1958, pp. 85 ff. S. A. Pletneva, *Ot Kochevii k Gorodam, Saltovo-Maiatskaya Kultura, MIA* 142, 1967; *Sb.Art.,* pp. 182–93.

Bibliography

COLLECTED WORKS

Cambridge Ancient History, vols: VIII, 1930; IX, 1932; XI, 1936; XII, 1939.

Cambridge Medieval History, vols: I, 1911; IV, 1929.

Drevnie Frakiytsy v Severnom Prichernomorie, Moscow 1939, *MIA* 150, eds T. D. Zlatkovskaya and A. I. Meliukova.

Issledovaniya po Arkheologii SSSR, Leningrad 1961 (*Prof. M. I. Artamonov Festschrift*) ed. V. F. Gaydukevich.

Istoria Rominiei, vol. I, Bucharest 1960.

Istoriya i Arkheologiya Yugo-Zapadnykh Oblastey SSSR Nachala Nashey Ery. Moscow 1967, *MIA* 139, eds B. A. Rybakov and E. A. Symonovich.

Istoriya SSSR, vol. I, Moscow 1966, eds S. A. Pletneva and B. A. Rybakov.

Kultura Drevnikh Skotovodov i Zemledeltsev Kazakhstana, Alma Ata 1969, ed. K. A. Akishev.

Materialy i Issledovaniya po Arkheologii SSSR, MIA, Moscow and Leningrad, in particular vols: 1, 1940; 23, 1951; 26, 1952; 36, 1954; 48, 1956; 60, 1959; 62, 1958; 64, 1958; 70, 1959; 78, 1960; 82, 1960; 88, 1960; 96, 1961; 98, 1961; 104, 1961; 115, 1962; 116, 1964; 142, 1967; 150, 1969; 151, 1969; 154, 1969.

Narysy Starodavnoy Istorii Ukrainskoy RSR, Kiev 1957, ed. S. M. Bibikov.

Novoe v Arkheologii Kazakhstana, Alma Ata 1968, ed. M. K. Kadyrbaev.

Ocherki Istorii SSSR, vol. I: *Pervobytno-Obshchynnyi Stroy i Drevneyshie Gosudarstva na Territorii SSSR*, Moscow 1957, eds P. N. Tretiakov and A. P. Mongait; vol. II: *Krizis Rabovladelcheskoy Sistemy i Zarozhdenie Feudalizma na Territorii SSSR*, III–IX vv., Moscow 1968, ed. B. A. Rybakov.

Real-Encyclopädie (Pauly-Wissowa), Stuttgart.

Voprosy Skifo-Sarmatskoy Arkheologii, Moscow 1954, ed. D. B. Shelov.

SELECT BIBLIOGRAPHY

ÅBERG, N., *Die Franken und Westgoten in der Völkerwanderungszeit,* Uppsala 1922.

ABETEKOV, A. K. and BARUZDIN, IU. D., *Arkheologicheskie Pamyatniki Talasskoy Doliny,* Frunze 1963.

AKISHEV, K. A. and KUSHAEV, G. A., *Drevnyaya Kultura Sakov i Usuney Doliny Reki Ili,* Alma Ata 1963.

ALFÖLDI, A. *Funde aus der Hunnenzeit und Ihre Ethnische Sonderung,* Budapest 1932, *AH* IX.

ALTHEIM, FR. *Weltgeschichte Asiens im Griechischen Zeitalter,* vol. II, Halle 1948.

— *Niedergang der Alten Welt,* vol. I, Frankfurt a.M. 1952.

AMBROZ, K. *Fibuly Iuga Evropeyskoy Chasti SSSR,* Moscow 1966.

ARTAMONOV, M. I. *Istoriya Khazar,* Leningrad 1962.

— *Sokrovishcha Skifskikh Kurganov,* Prague 1966.

— *Treasures from Scythian Tombs,* London 1969.

BARLOEWEN, W. D. VON *Abriss der Geschichte Antiker Randkulturen,* Munich 1961.

BENINGER, E. *Der Westgotisch-Alanische Zug nach Mitteleuropa,* Leipzig 1931.

BLAVATSKII, V. A. *Antichnaya Arkheologiya Severnogo Prichernomorya,* Moscow 1961.

BOLTON, J. D. P. *Aristeas of Proconnesus,* Oxford 1962.

BURY, J. B. *History of the Later Roman Empire (AD 395–565),* 2 vols, London 1923, New York 1957.

CHERNIKOV, S. S. *Zagadka Zolotogo Kurgana,* Moscow 1965.

CSALÁNY, D. *Archäologische Denkmäler der Gepiden im Mitteldonau-becken (454–568 u.Z.),* Budapest 1961, *AH* SN XXXVIII.

CULICAN, W. *The Medes and Persians,* London and New York, 1965.

CZEKANOWSKI, J. *Wstep do Historii Słowian,* 2nd ed., Poznań 1957.

DALTON, O. M. *The Treasure of the Oxus,* London 1926, rpr. 1964.

DIACONU, G. *Tîrgişor—Necropola din Secolele III–IV e.n.,* Bucharest 1965.

DICULESCU, C. C. *Die Wandalen und die Goten in Ungarn und Rumänien,* Leipzig 1923.

DVORNIK, F. *The Making of Central and Eastern Europe,* London 1949.
— *The Slavs. Their Early History and Civilisation,* Boston 1956.
EBERT, M. *Südrussland im Altertum,* rpr. Bonn 1960.
FETTICH, N. *Der Zweite Schatz von Szilágysomlyó,* Budapest 1932, *AH* VII.
— *Archäologische Studien zur Geschichte der Späthunnischen Metallkunst,* Budapest 1951, *AH* XXXI.
— *La Trouvaille de Tombe Princière Hunnique à Szeged-Nagyszékós,* Budapest 1953, *AH* XXXII.
FILIP, J. *Keltové ve Střední Evropě,* Prague 1956, Monumenta Archaeo-logica V.
GAGOLOYTI, Iu. S. *Alany i Voprosy Etnogeneza Osetii,* Tbilisi 1966.
GAYDUKEVICH, V. F. *Bosporskoe Tsarstvo,* Moscow and Leningrad 1948.
GHIRSHMAN, R. *Iran: The Parthians and Sassanians,* London 1962.
— *Persia, from the Origins to Alexander the Great,* London 1964.
HARMATTA, J. *Studies on the History of the Sarmatians,* Budapest 1950.
ILINSKAYA, V. A. *Skify Dneprovskogo Lesostepnogo Levoberezhya,* Kiev 1968.
JETMAR, K. *Art of the Steppes. The Eurasian Animal Style,* London 1967.
KISELEV, S. V. *Drevnyaya Istoriya Iuzhnoy Sibiri,* Moscow 1951.
KLOSE, J. *Roms Klientel-Randstaaten am Rhein und an der Donau,* Breslau 1934.
KNIPOVICH, T. N. *Tanais,* Moscow and Leningrad 1949.
KONDAKOV, N. P., TOLSTOY, I. I. and REINACH, S. *Antiquités de la Russie Meridionale,* Paris 1891.
KOSTRZEWSKI, J., CHMIELEWSKI, W. and JAŻDŻEWSKI, K. *Pradzieje Polski,* Wrocław, Warsaw and Cracow 1965.
KOVPANENKO, H. T. *Plemena Skifskoho Chasu na Vorskli,* Kiev 1967.
KROPOTKIN, V. V. *Klady Rimskikh Monet na Territorii SSSR,* Moscow 1961.
— *Ekonomicheskie Svyazi Vostochnoy Evropy v I Tysyacheletii N.E.,* Moscow 1967.
KRUGLIKOVA, I. T. *Bospor v Pozdneantichnoe Vremya,* Moscow 1966.
KUKHARENKO, Iu. V. *Zarubinetskaya Kultura,* Moscow 1964.
KUZNETSOV, A. V. *Arkheologicheskie Raskopki v Rayone Zhmeyskoy, Severnoy Osetii,* Ordzhonikidze 1961.

KYZLASOV, L. R. *Tashtykskaya Epokha v Istorii Khakassko-Minusinskoy Kotloviny,* Moscow 1960.

LIBEROV, P. D. *Pamyatniki Skifskogo Vremeni na Srednem Donu,* Moscow 1965.

LJAPUSHKIN, I. I. *Dneprovskoe Lesostepnoe Levoberezhye v Epokhu Zheleza,* 1961, *MIA* 104.

ŁOWMIAŃSKI, H. *Początki Polski,* vol. I, Warsaw 1963; vol. II, 1964.

MATTINGLY, H. and SYDENHAM, E. A. *The Roman Imperial Coinage,* vol. III, London 1930.

MELIUKOVA, A. I. *Vooruzhenie Skifov,* Moscow 1964.

MILLER, M. A. *Don i Priazovie v Drevnosti,* part II, Munich 1958.

MINNS, E. H. *Scythians and Greeks,* Cambridge 1913, rpr. 1965.

MITREA, C. and PREDA, C. *Necropole din Secolul al IV-lea E.N. in Muntenia,* Bucharest 1966.

MONGAIT, A. L. *Archaeology in the U.S.S.R.,* trans. by M. W. Thompson, Harmondsworth 1961.

MOSHKOVA, M. G. *Pamyatniki Prokhorovskoy Kultury,* Moscow 1963.

NALEPA, J. *Die Grundlagen und der Zerfall der nordwestslawischen Spracheinheit,* in Polish with a summary in German, Poznań 1968.

PARDUCZ, M. Denkmäler der Sarmatenzeit in Ungarn, Budapest: part I *AH* XXV, 1941; part II *AH* XXVIII, 1944; part III *AH* XXX, 1950; part IV *AAASH* VII., 1956.

— *Die Ethnischen Probleme der Hunnenzeit in Ungarn,* Budapest 1963.

PARVAN, V. *Dacia. An Outline of the Early Civilisations of the Carpatho-Danubian Countries,* Oxford 1928.

PASTERNAK, IA. *Arkheologiya Ukrainy,* Toronto 1961.

PETRENKO, V. G. *Pravoberezhie Srednego Pridneprovya v V-III vv. do n.e.,* Moscow 1967.

RIKMAN, E. A. *Pamyatnik Epokhi Velikogo Pereseleniya Narodov,* Budeshty, Kishinev 1967.

ROSTOVTSEV, M. *Iranians and Greeks in South Russia,* Oxford 1922.

— *The Animal Style in South Russia and China,* Princeton 1929.

— *Skythien und der Bosporus,* Berlin 1931.

RUDENKO, S. I. *Kultura Naseleniya Tsentralnogo Altaya v Skifskoe Vremya,* Moscow and Leningrad 1960.

— *Sibirskaya Kollektsiya Petra I,* Moscow and Leningrad 1962.

— *Kultura Khunnov i Noinulinskie Kurgany,* Moscow and Leningrad 1962.

SCHMIDT, B. *Die Späte Völkerwanderungzeit in Mitteldeutschland,* Halle 1961.

SCHMIDT, L. *Geschichte der Deutschen Stämme,* I Abteilung, Berlin 1910.

SHELOV, D. B. *Nekropol Tanaisa,* Moscow 1961, *MIA* 98.

SHOVKOPLYAS, I. G. *Arkheologichni Doslidzhennya na Ukraini (1917–1957),* Kiev 1957.

SMIRNOV, A. P. *Skify,* Moscow 1966.

SMIRNOV, K. F. *Vooruzhenie Savromatov,* Moscow 1961, *MIA* 101.

— Savromaty. *Rannyaya Istoriya i Kultura Sarmatov,* Moscow 1964.

SMIRNOV, K. F. and PETRENKO, V. G. *Savromaty Povolzhya i Yuzhnogo Priuralya,* Moscow 1963.

SOLOMONIK, E. I. *Sarmatskie Znaki Severnogo Prichenomoria,* Kiev 1959.

SULIMIRSKI, T. *The Scythians in West Podolia,* in Polish with a summary in German, Lwów 1936.

— Scythian Antiquities in Central Europe. *The Antiquaries Journal,* XXV, London 1945, pp. 1–11.

— Les Archers à Cheval—Cavalerie Légère des Anciens. *Revue Internationale d'Histoire Militaire,* vol. 3, No. 12, Paris 1952, pp. 447–61.

— Scythian Antiquities in Western Asia. *Artibus Asiae,* vol. XVII, Ascona 1954, pp. 282–318.

— Scythian Notes. *Palaeologia,* vol. IV, Osaka 1955, pp. 281–4.

— The Cimmerian Problem, *Bulletin* No. 2, 1960, pp. 45–64. See also Cimmerians, *Encyclopaedia Britannica,* vol. 5, 1963, p. 773.

— Die Skythen in Mittel- und Westeuropa, *Bericht über den V. Kongress f. Vor- und Frühgeschichte,* Hamburg 1958, Berlin 1961, pp. 793–99.

— The Forgotten Sarmatians, chap. XII in *Vanished Civilisations,* London 1963.

— Sarmatians in the Polish Past, *The Polish Review,* vol. IX–I, New York, pp. 13–66.

— The Find from Zamość and its Background, in Polish with a summary in English, *Archeologia Polski,* vol. XI, Warsaw 1966, pp. 118–73; and its short version in English: An Important Find from Eastern Poland, *Antiquity,* vol. XL, No. 159, 1966, pp. 221–3, pl. 38–9.

— The Problem of the West-Volhynian Centre of the 3rd–4th Centuries AD. *Reports of the I International Congress of Slavonic Archaeology,* Warsaw 1965. Vol. II, Warsaw 1969, pp. 268–77, in Polish with a summary in English.

The Sarmatians

— Ancient Southern Neighbours of the Baltic Tribes, *Acta Baltico-Slavica*, vol V, Białystok 1967, pp. 1–17.

— The Bronze Age of the USSR—A Guide to the Recent Literature on the Subject, *Bulletin* No. 7 1968, pp. 43–83.

— The Late Bronze Age and Early Iron Age of the USSR—A Guide to the Recent Literature on the Subject, *Bulletin* No. 8, 1969.

— *Prehistoric Russia*, London 1970.

TALBOT RICE, T. *The Scythians*, 3rd ed. London 1961.

TCHLENOVA, N. L. *Proiskhozhdenie i Rannyaya Istoria Plemen Tagarskoy Kultury*, Moscow 1967.

TERENOZHKIN, A. I. *Predskifskii Period na Dneprovskom Pravoberezhie*, Kiev 1961.

THOMPSON, E. A. *A History of Attila and the Huns*, Oxford 1948.

TOLSTOV, S. P. *Drevniy Khorezm*, Moscow 1948.

— *Po Drevnim Deltam Oksa i Yaksarta*, Moscow 1962.

TRETIAKOV, P. N. *Vostochnoslavyanskie Plemena*, 2nd ed., Moscow 1953.

VASILEV, A. A. *The Goths in the Crimea*, Cambridge, Mass. 1936.

VERNADSKY, G. *Ancient Russia*, New Haven 1944.

VULPE, R. *The Ancient History of Dobrogea*, Bucharest 1940.

— *Izvoare. Sapaturile din 1936–1948*. Bucharest 1957.

VYAZMITINA, M. I. *Zolota Balka*, Kiev 1962.

WERNER, J. *Beiträge zur Archäologie des Attila Reiches*, Munich 1956.

— *Katalog der Sammlung Diergardt (Völkerwanderungszeitlicher Schmuck)*, Berlin 1961.

ZAEHNER, R. C. *The Dawn and Twilight of Zoroastrianism*, London 1961.

ZEISS, H. *Die Grabfunde aus dem Spanischen Westgotenreich*, Berlin and Leipzig 1934. Germanische Denkmäler der Völkerwanderungszeit II.

ZGUSTA, L. *Die Personennamen Griechischer Städte der Nördlichen Schwarzmeerküste*, Prague 1955.

1

2

3

4

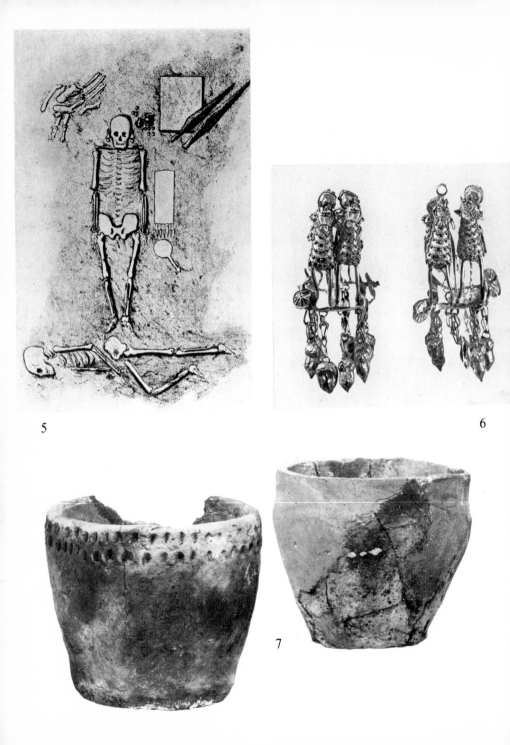

5

6

7

8

9

10

11

13

12

14

15

16

17

18

21

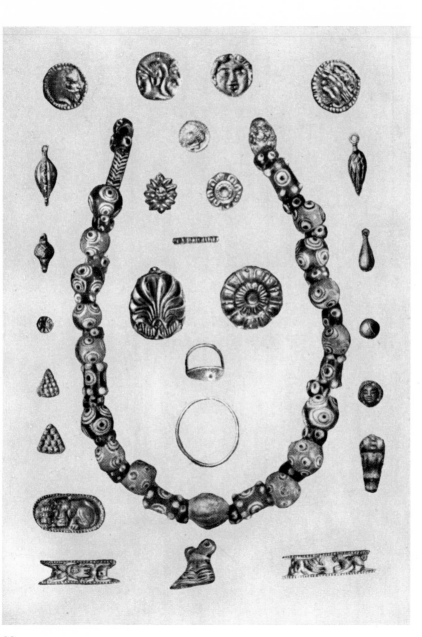

24

23

25

26

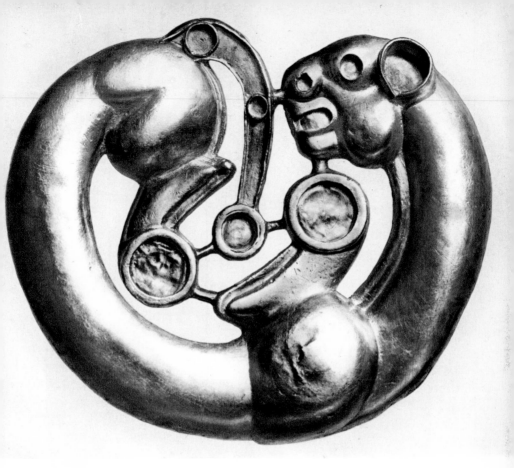

27

28

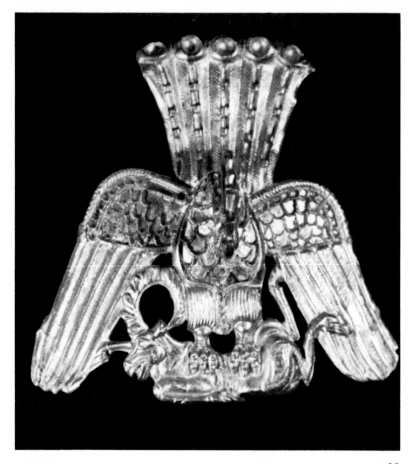

29

30

31

32

33

34

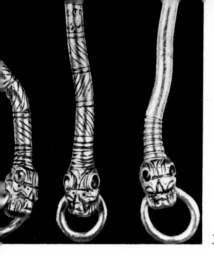

35

36

37

38

39

40

42

43

44

45

46

47

50

51

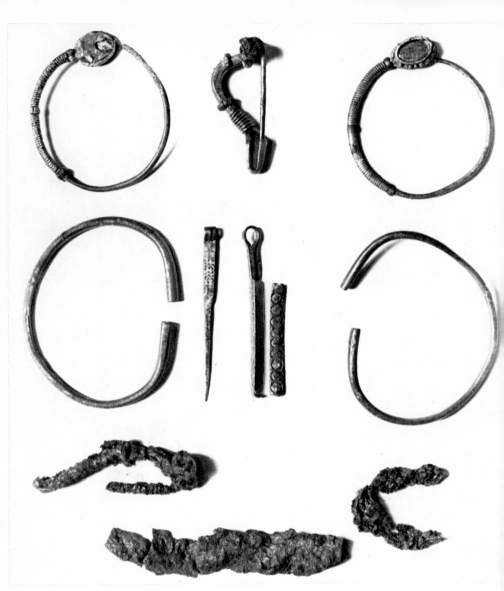

52

54

55

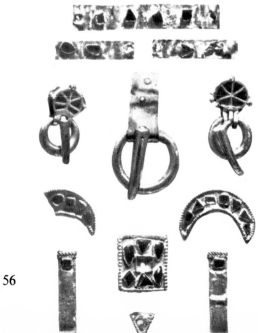

56

57

58

59

60

Notes on the Plates

1, 2 Gold plaques from the Oxus treasure, each with the figure of a Sacian (Scythian) holding divining rods. *c.* 400 BC. British Museum.

3 Amyrgian Sacians bringing tribute to the Persian king. A bas-relief in the palace of Xerxes at Persepolis. Fifth century BC.

4 Sarmatian (Roxolanian) detachment of the cataphracti fleeing from the Roman cavalry. From Trajan's Column in Rome.

5 Burial of an armed Sarmatian woman accompanied by an attendant. Fourth century BC. Kholodnyi Yar on the Tjasmin, Ukraine; barrow grave no. 20.

6 Gold pendants (ornaments for the temples) in the shape of mounted horsemen, the horses presumably drawing a chariot. Found in a Sauro-matian princely barrow grave of the fifth century BC at Sazonkin Bugor, near Chernyi Yar on the lower Volga. Astrakhan Museum.

7 Two Sauromatian clay vessels of 'flower-pot' type from Verkhnee-Pogromnoe near Volgograd (lower Volga group). Hermitage Museum, Leningrad.

8 Bone plaque in the shape of a panther, part of a horse harness, from the Sauromatian barrow grave 8, burial 1, at Verkhnee-Pogromnoe near Volgograd. Hermitage Museum, Leningrad.

9 Winged griffin, forming the terminal of a torque, from Siberia. Hermit-age Museum, Leningrad.

10 Gold plaque in openwork from Siberia. The seated woman represents a European racial type, whereas a Mongoloid admixture is recognizable

in the faces of both men. The headdress of the woman calls to mind the wooden helmet worn by the woman buried in the fifth-century BC barrow grave 5 at Pazyryk. The figures represented on the plaques may have been of the Tagarskaya culture stock. Original in the Hermitage Museum, Leningrad.

11, 12 Pottery characteristic of the Prokhorovka culture, from Novo-Nikol-skoe, barrow grave 9, burial 2 and Nizhne-Vodyanoe, barrow 3, grave 3, both near Volgograd. Hermitage Museum, Leningrad.

13 Clay vessel from Kalinovka, barrow grave 55, burial 8. Middle Sarmatian period.

14–16 Iron daggers of the Prokhorovka culture from graves in the Volgograd region: Srednaya Akhtuba barrow 2, burial 7 and barrow 8, burial 8; and Verkhnee-Pogromnoe barrow 7, burial 9.

17 Glass amphora of Egyptian make from Kerch (Panticapaeum). Late sixth-fifth century BC. National Museum, Warsaw.

18 Glass amphora of Syrian manufacture, found in the North Pontic area. Late sixth century BC. National Museum, Warsaw.

19 Gold bracelet with terminals in the shape of lions' heads, from the Kul-Oba princely barrow grave near Kerch in the Crimea. Original in the Hermitage Museum, Leningrad.

20 Gold vase from the Kul-Oba burial, showing a Scythian stringing a bow. Fourth century BC. Original in the Hermitage Museum, Leningrad.

21 Gold cover of a bow-case (gorytus) from the royal barrow grave at Melitopol. Fourth century BC.

22 Personal gold ornaments and paste beads from the female burial in the royal barrow grave at Melitopol. Fourth century BC.

23, 24 Golden spiral armlet and bracelet with zoomorphic terminals, from Verkhnee-Pogromnoe near Volgograd, barrow grave 5, burial 2. Hermitage Museum, Leningrad.

25 Golden spiral armlet with zoomorphic terminals, from barrow grave 55, burial 2, at Kalinovka near Volgograd. Hermitage Museum, Leningrad.

26 Gold spiral bracelet with zoomorphic terminals from Kalinovka near Volgograd, barrow grave 55, burial 8. The objects shown in plates 23–26 belong to the Middle Sarmatian period: second century BC to mid-first century AD. Hermitage Museum, Leningrad.

27 Massive gold plaque representing a panther twisted into a circle. The eye, nostril, ear, claws and tail were originally inlaid. From Siberia, *c.* 400 BC. Hermitage Museum, Leningrad.

28 Gold torque from Siberia with terminals in the shape of lions' heads, their eyes, ears and the corners of their lower jaw set with turquoise. Hermitage Museum, Leningrad.

29 Gold plaque in the form of a griffin-eagle with its prey, an ibex. The tops of the eagle's wings and the eye of the ibex were inlaid with red glass, and the body of the ibex was inlaid with blue paste. From Siberia. Original in the Hermitage Museum, Leningrad.

30 Gold plaque from Siberia representing a doe attacked by two rapacious animals. The figures are inlaid with paste and coloured glass. Hermitage Museum, Leningrad.

31 Pottery from a barrow grave at Stanitsa Marievskaya, Kuban, north-west Caucasus. Third-second century BC. Hermitage Museum, Leningrad.

32 Terracotta figure of Kybele found in the Bosporan (Greek) town of Mirmekia in the Crimea. Second century BC. This Bosporan deity probably derived from the goddess of all animals worshipped by the Greeks in Asia Minor. Kybele's worship was later adopted by some

Scythian and Sarmatian tribes, by whom she was regarded as the goddess of all nature. Representations of her are frequent in Scytho-Sarmatian art. National Museum, Warsaw.

33 Marble stele of Triphon found in Tanais, the Bosporan city at the mouth of the Don. The knight is dressed in true Sarmatian fashion. Hermitage Museum, Leningrad.

34 Gold diadem set with garnets from Besleneevskaya Stanitsa in the north-west Caucasus; masterpiece of a Greek goldsmith of the Middle Sarmatian period. Hermitage Museum, Leningrad.

35 Zoomorphic terminals of gold neck-rings from a hoard at Largutse on the Pruth, Bessarabia, representing types current in the fourth-third centuries BC.

36 Silver phalera from the North Pontic area, exact provenance unknown. Second century BC. Bibliothèque Nationale, Cabinet des Médailles, Paris.

37 Bronze belt-buckles from Kerch (Panticapaeum) ornamented with a tamga sign in openwork. British Museum.

38 Stone block from Krivoy Rog in the Ukraine covered with tamga signs engraved at different periods: the tamgas show every stage of development. Museum of Archaeology, Odessa.

39 Small bronze mirror with a tamga sign cast on the back. North Pontic steppe. Museum für Vor- u. Frühgeschichte, Berlin.

40 Large bronze cauldron from the region between the Don and the Donets, bearing a cast tamga sign. Historical Museum, Moscow.

41-43 Objects from the burial of a Sarmatian queen at Novocherkassk: gold coronet inlaid with precious stones; gold jug with a stag handle; gold bowl with zoomorphic handles; gold needle box and two perfume boxes, one with the lid secured by a gold chain and all covered with repoussé decoration. Hermitage Museum, Leningrad.

44 Reconstructed bust of the Sarmatian queen from Novocherkassk.

45 Roman coins bearing the title 'Sarmaticus' (SARM) taken by Roman emperors after victories over the Hungarian Sarmatians. Top: obverse of an aureus of Marcus Aurelius; the other two from the reign of Commodus (issued AD 177–8), with reverse types showing stylized barbarian armour as trophies. British Museum.

46 Damaged funeral stele from the Roman camp at Chester, with the figure, carved in relief, of a mounted Sarmatian chief, clad in scale armour, of possible Roxolanian ancestry. Chester Museum.

47 Iron dagger with a ring pommel set with a glass bead, found in grave 143 at Szentes-Kistoke. Middle Sarmatian period in Hungary. Szentes Museum.

48, 49 Beads, bronze brooches, rings, golden plaques, etc., found in Early Sarmatian graves in Hungary: first and second centuries AD. Szentes Museum.

50 Necklaces of different types of beads and a perforated shell pendant, from grave 112 at Kiszombor B. Late Sarmatian period in Hungary. Szentes Museum.

51 Collection of objects, the so-called 'herdsman's bag' (iron knife, awl, strike-a-light, flint and whetstone) and a necklace, found in grave 73 at Kiszombor B. Late Sarmatian period in Hungary. Szentes Museum.

52 Bronze bracelets, bronze and iron brooches and other objects from graves at Szentes-Jaksor. Late Sarmatian period in Hungary. Szentes Museum.

53 Silver-gilt shield-boss of Germanic type with Sarmatian ornament, from a Sarmatian princely burial at Herpály in north-east Hungary. Third century AD. Original in the Hungarian National Historical Museum.

54-56   Personal ornaments and other objects from the burial of a Hunnic governor, presumably of Sarmatian-Alanic stock, found at Jakuszo- wice, north of Cracow, in Poland. Found in the same grave were the man's sword and a golden bow, his insignia of rank, shown in fig. 72. Archaeological Museum, Cracow.

57, 58   Three silver Sarmatian plate brooches of 'Gothic' type, found in the region of Troyes in northern France. Troyes Museum.

59   Silver hoard from Martinovka in the Ukraine, presumably the property of a ruling family of the Antae, Slavicised descendants of the Alanic Antae, overrun by the Turkic Avars *c.* AD 600. The strap-end at the bottom bears late tamga signs. British Museum.

60   Silver cover of a wooden scabbard from a late Alanic (eleventh-twelfth century) 'catacomb' grave at Zmeyskaya in northern Ossetia in the Caucasus. The silver cover is richly decorated and inlaid with garnets and almandines. Institute of Archaeology, Moscow.